THE NEW RULES FOR

LOVE SEX & DATING

D0029006

ANDY STANLEY

ZONDERVAN®

ZONDERVAN

The New Rules for Love, Sex, and Dating
Copyright © 2014 by Andy Stanley

Requests for information should be addressed to:
Zondervan, 3900 *Sparks Dr. SE, Grand Rapids, Michigan 49546*

ISBN 978-0-310-34450-6 (audio)

ISBN 978-0-310-34220-5 (ebook)

Library of Congress Cataloging-in-Publication Data

Stanley, Andy.
     The new rules for love, sex, and dating / Andy Stanley. — 1st [edition].
      pages cm
     ISBN 978-0-310-34219-9 (softcover)
     1. Sex — Religious aspects — Christianity. 2. Dating (Social customs) — Religious
    aspects — Christianity. 3. Love — Religious aspects — Christianity. I. Title.
    BT708.S825   2015
    241'.664 — dc23   2014040217

All Scripture quotations, unless otherwise indicated, are taken from The Holy Bible, New International Version®, NIV®. Copyright © 1973, 1978, 1984, 2011 by Biblica, Inc.® Used by permission. All rights reserved worldwide. www.Zondervan.com. The "NIV" and "New International Version" are trademarks registered in the United Stated Patent and Trademark office by Biblica, Inc.®

Scripture quotations marked KJV are taken from *The Holy Bible, King James Version.* Public domain.

Scripture quotations marked NASB are taken from the *New American Standard Bible.®* Copyright © 1960, 1962, 1963, 1968, 1971, 1972, 1973, 1975, 1977, 1995 by The Lockman Foundation. Used by permission. (www.Lockman.org)

Any Internet addresses (websites, blogs, etc.) and telephone numbers in this book are offered as a resource. They are not intended in any way to be or imply an endorsement by the author or Zondervan, nor does the author or Zondervan vouch for the content of these sites and numbers for the life of this book.

All rights reserved. No part of this publication may be reproduced, stored in a retrieval system, or transmitted in any form or by any means — electronic, mechanical, photocopy, recording, or any other — except for brief quotations in printed reviews, without the prior permission of the publisher.

Cover photography: © *MaxyM / Shutterstock®*
Interior design: Beth Shagene

First Printing November 2014 / Printed in the United States of America

*To my friends from 4th and Peachtree
who carried their HFITFC
all the way to the altar.*

CONTENTS

ACKNOWLEDGMENTS

In 1986 I was handed the reins of a struggling youth group attached to a flourishing downtown church in the city of Atlanta. It was there, on the corner of 4th and Peachtree, that I gave my first talk on the subject matter contained in these pages. The teenagers who put up with me as I honed my communication skills have teenagers of their own now. Many of them are friends. A handful work with me. To those of you who remember or perhaps still have your original copy of the *How Far Is Too Far Chart*, thank you. Sandra and I often comment that those were perhaps the best and most productive years of our lives.

To John Raymond at Zondervan, thank you. Your instant enthusiasm around this content is a big part of why I considered tackling this project in the first place. While I insisted it had all been said before, you convinced me it needed to be said *again*. Thank you.

As most authors know, it's easy to start a book. Finishing is another story. When it comes to publishing, Suzy Gray is the reason I finish what I start. Thank you, Suzy. Thank you for your attention to detail. Thank you for reading, rereading, and reading again. You make things better. You certainly made this book better.

Finally, thank you, Sandra. Thank you for the nights and mornings you walked quietly through the house when you knew I was in my zone. Thank you for listening when I felt compelled to read out loud. Thank you for the occasional "I don't think you should say that." I didn't. I'm more in love with you than ever. If I knew then what I know now, I would marry you again, only sooner!

INTRODUCTION

I have three children, two boys and a girl. They're all in college. If you're reading this book three or more years after the original publication date, I hope they're out by now. But as of this afternoon, they're all tucked away in a library studying their hearts out. I hope.

When my sons got to the magic age when traditional fathers have the traditional *talk*, I informed them we were going to handle the situation a bit differently. Instead of an awkward fifteen-*minute* talk, we were going to begin an awkward fifteen-*year* conversation. And we did. Why this approach? Well, most boys are introduced to the topic of sex before they are actually interested in sex. By the time they're actually interested in sex, they've forgotten all those fascinating insights their fathers shared. Every year or two requires some review and something new. So I did my best to keep the conversation alive and current.

It's still a bit awkward at times. But we make eye contact now. I assured them early on that transparency in matters related to love, sex, and dating wouldn't land them in "time out" or worse. Everybody struggles. Everybody faces similar temptations. Everybody has regrets. So as we begin this awkward journey together, I thought it might be helpful to begin with some of the stuff my grown-up children and I talk about. Stuff we've all observed. For example, we live in a highly sexualized culture. Images in contemporary advertisements are more graphic than previous generations' pornography. Sex is leveraged to sell just about everything. Actually, the promise of *no-strings-attached sex* with a *way-above-average-looking person* is used to sell just about everything. Sexual scandals among politicians, athletes, and celebrities elicit yawns. Infidelity is woven into the plot of just about every form of entertainment that involves a plot.

Nothing new there. But it does remind me of one of my finer parenting moments.

When Andrew, our oldest, was in ninth grade, everybody was watching *The Office*. Everybody. No freshmen dared show their faces at Milton High School if they were not conversant with the previous evening's episode. You think I'm exaggerating. On many occasions, Andrew got up an hour early to watch the show before school because his unreasonable parents made him study instead of watching television the night before. We were so hard core.

Like most everything on television, *The Office* was laced with sexual innuendo. Sometimes more lace than innuendo. This bothered his mother and me. We wrestled with the issue of age-appropriate entertainment. Andrew assured me on multiple occasions that *The Office* was clean and I didn't need to worry. So I decided to use *The Office* to introduce and hopefully sensitize Andrew to the sexual subtleties of prime-time television.

I handed him a pen and a 3" x 5" card and told him I wanted him to watch one episode sitting beside his mom and to make a slash mark for every sexual reference. He agreed. Silly parents.

I walked in a few minutes after the show started. They were still flashing up the opening credits. Andrew already had five marks on his card. Sandra gave me that, "Seriously, we're letting our son watch this?" look. Andrew was horrified. "Dad, it's never like this. I promise. Does Mom really have to sit here the whole time?"

The Flip Side

The reason I bother to mention our march toward the sexualization of everything is that it stands in stark contrast to a second cultural current of which we're all aware. One that's been around since the beginning of time. Namely, a deep appreciation of and desire for good ol' fashioned, stand-the-test-of-time love. *And they lived happily ever after* isn't a line used much anymore, but it could certainly be tacked on to just about every chick flick. Isn't that what makes a chick flick a chick flick? Add to that the plethora of online matchmaking services, along with a growing list of reality TV shows built around helping individuals navigate their relational options. So while we are a culture enamored with the idea of unencumbered, consequence-free sex, we can't seem to abandon our infatuation with long-term relational exclusivity either.

What's a girl to do?

At this juncture you might expect me to lay the blame for our cultural duplicity at the feet of your favorite actress, recording artist, and everybody else on the West Coast, who many believe are responsible for creating our sex-crazed culture. But I'm not that guy and this isn't that book. I'm not all that interested in *why* things are the way they are. I'm more interested in helping you navigate the way things are. My purpose in writing is to increase your relational satisfaction quota. Because sex is usually part of long-term relationships, we're going to talk about sex. But we're going to talk about it within a larger context than a single relationship or a single event. As much as culture tries to separate our sexual experiences from the rest of our lives, it can't be done.

I bet you already knew that.

Perhaps you've already tried that.

We're going to talk about love. We're going to explore what it means to love someone and what it takes for someone to love us back. We're going to explore love that includes, but goes beyond, chemistry. Along the way I hope to restore your belief that marriage can last a lifetime.

Some of what I have to say will be painful. Some of it you won't believe. You'll be tempted to close your book (or return to the home screen of your mobile device). I'm going to challenge some assumptions. I'm going to remind you of some unwise choices and bad decisions. Though my intent is neither to judge nor condemn you, you may feel both before we're finished. As negative as all that sounds, by the end of the first chapter I believe you'll believe I have your best interest at heart. I want something *for* you, not *from* you. Relationally speaking, I want for you what you want for you. Namely, *more*. As you've discovered, our highly sexualized culture does not deliver on its promise. It can't. Truth is, what our sexually liberated culture offers is ultimately not all that liberating.

How do I know?

Confession Magnet

As you may know, I'm a pastor. Like most pastors, I'm somewhat of a walking conscience. Because of the size of our congregation I'm pretty well known in our community. People who've never met me feel like they know me. So it's common for folks to walk up to me at the mall or in a coffee shop and just start talking. Seriously, no introduction; they just start talking. Before they know it, they've opened the vaults of their souls and invited me to step inside. Actually, I don't have to step inside. They bring everything out and put it on display like a garage sale. Everything.

It usually begins with, "You're Andy, aren't you? Well, my wife ... my husband ... my marriage ... my boyfriend ... my girlfriend ... my past ..." They launch into personal, detailed stories with little or no filter. I'm thinking, *You shouldn't tell anybody this, much less your pastor, in public!*

But they do. In one unfiltered purge. Then I go home and share their stories with my kids. Experience is a brutal teacher. I figure my kids should learn all they can from other people's experience.

When I can, I stop them and say, "Okay, hold on one second; perhaps we should start with a name." And those are the face-to-face encounters. You should read my mail and email. Fine print. Single-spaced. Pages and pages. Lurid details. Extraordinary pain and regret. In the majority of cases there is a sexual/relational component. As I listen or read, I think,

Really?

Didn't you see that coming?

Didn't you know that ... ?

Did no one ever tell you that ... ?

Did your momma never sit you down and explain that if you ... ?

Don't you understand how men think?

Don't you know what women need?

Don't you understand the way life is?

After years of this I've concluded that for most people the answer is no to most of those questions. Nobody told 'em. Nobody warned 'em. Nobody taught 'em. For whatever reason, Mom and Dad skipped some really important information. They had the *talk* and then went back to *Dancing with the Stars.*

So, while I don't have all the answers, I have *some* answers. And while I won't fill your cup in the pages that follow, I intend to empty mine. I'll do my best to address as many of the aforementioned "Didn't you know?" questions I can.

For the sake of full disclosure, you should know I'm not

a psychologist. I don't hold a PhD in anything. Not only am I not a doctor, I didn't even make nurse. So other than my retail, coffee shop, and hallway confessions, what qualifies me to delve into your personal life? Nothing really. I'm not writing because I'm *qualified*. I'm writing because I'm *concerned*. I'm not a licensed counselor. Counselors are required to listen. I'm not that patient. Besides, the way I see it, there are only three or four life narratives. Once I've identified which one an individual has opted for or fallen into, I'm ready to start dispensing advice. People don't like it when I interrupt their stories before they're finished. Know why? They think their stories are original. Unique. Chances are, so do you.

So let me go ahead and burst the first of many bubbles. While it's true that you're a one-of-a-kind person, your story is not a one-of-a-kind story; it's original to you, but it's not original. And that's a good thing. The fact that your story isn't original is what makes it possible for someone like me to offer advice and suggest a new approach. If you embrace the myths that *your* story is a story unto itself, that *your* experience is unique to you, and that *your* love life is like no one else's, then you will find it easy to dismiss everything I'm about to suggest. You'll see yourself as the exception to every *rule*. While it's true that you're *exceptional*, you are not an *exception*. It's this disturbing discovery that moves the fifty-plus crowd in our churches to cheer me on whenever I address this topic. They've lived long enough to recognize just how unexceptional we all really are.

I've been married twenty-seven years — to the same

person. That says more about Sandra than it does about me. My parents divorced after thirty-something years of a less-than-ideal marriage. Most couples would have given up way sooner. Sandra's parents seem to be as in love as the day they met. So I've seen a lot. Good and bad. I've learned a lot. I've been teaching the principles I'm about to share with you long enough to see results. I've received hundreds, maybe thousands, of letters, emails, and texts from people who say they wish they'd heard what I'm about to share with you when they were in their twenties; before their first marriage; before they reached for the divorce lever. Whenever I share this content, the response is overwhelming. The group that cheers me on with the most enthusiasm is parents. They want their dating-age kids to avoid the mistakes they made. They hope their kids will get it right the first time. I can't tell you how many parents of preschoolers and elementary-aged kids have purchased audio and video versions of this material to save for their children when they are old enough to need it.

So whether you're *still* in or *back* in a season of looking for the love of your life, I can help. If you're living with someone in an attempt to discover whether he or she is the right choice of a lifetime companion, this content will help. If you've given up on love or if you've never seen a marriage you would be caught dead in, this content may very well restore your hope. If you've concluded, "All guys are the same," and "Women only care about how much a guy makes," keep reading.

However, if you're a recreational or serial dater, if you're a *player*, if you're recently divorced and plan to spend the next few years living your adolescent dreams, you may have wasted your money or somebody else's. For that, there's eBay. Or, just put this on a shelf for the time being. You may want to dust it off at a later date.

Looking Ahead

One thing that makes this topic a bit tricky is that sex and our sexuality are a bit like fire. Fire in its proper context is very appealing. Out of its proper context, it's extremely destructive. The same is true for all things sexual. If you've never been married or are under thirty, even if you've lived with someone, you underestimate the complexity of your sexuality and the long-term ramifications of your sexual conduct. You don't underestimate because you aren't smart. You underestimate because of your birthday and life experience — two things you have little or no control over. So it's not your fault. One thing I hope to do during our pages together is to reframe the subject of sex in such a way that you see it for what it is. Suffice it to say, "it" is both wonderful and powerful. The wonderful part makes it worth pursuing. The powerful part makes it worth respecting. It's a lack of respect for one's sexuality that sets up a lot of the thirty-and-older crowd for unintended confusion and relational chaos.

More on that later.

Future Perfect

I'm hoping our time together will empower you to avoid what I know you would love to avoid. In most contexts, information is power. The arena of love, sex, and dating is no exception. If you've never been married, you get to get it right the first time. If you are single again, perhaps the following pages will empower you to keep the painful aspects of your history from repeating themselves. The present, what you're doing right now, will eventually be part of your past. The past, especially your relational past, has a pesky way of showing up at the most inopportune times in your future. I've met with many struggling married couples who would describe themselves as having "marriage problems." But in all my years I've never talked to a married couple that actually had a *marriage* problem. What I've discovered is that people with problems get married and their problems collide. What was manageable as a single person eventually becomes unmanageable within the context of marriage. Marriage problems are easy. They rarely require counseling. But when the premarriage past surfaces in a marriage, that's another story. That dynamic is one of the primary reasons I wrote this book. There's enough unavoidable pain in life. I want to help you avoid the avoidable pain. Namely, pain you will experience later because of decisions you are making right now.

Here we go.

CHAPTER 1

THE RIGHT PERSON MYTH

At the center of every great love story are two people who are *right* for each other, destined to be together. We're usually able to spot 'em three or four scenes into a movie or a half-dozen chapters into a novel. You just know. Usually before they do. Three hundred pages or a hundred and twenty minutes later they've figured out what we knew all along, leaving us entertained and, in some cases, inspired by their story.

Then there's *The Bachelor* and *The Bachelorette*. In the case of these two reality TV shows, we don't know who's *right* for whom until the end. We think we do. That's what makes it so entertaining. But in the end, regardless of how many potential *right* candidates there are, one and only one is chosen. The *right* one.

Hopefully.

I say "hopefully" because every hardcore *B'* and *B'ette* fan scans the Internet for weeks following that final episode to see who was *right* after all. As of the writing of this book, it appears that five contestants chose well. The others? They moved on to the next *right* person.

I realize that you realize movies, reality TV, and novels don't reflect real life. I assume you don't take your relationship cues from script writers and authors. But it's possible you've embraced the underlying premise that holds these story lines and episodes together. That assumption being: *there's a right person for you, and once you find your right person, everything will be all right.*

I call this The Right Person Myth.

The myth isn't, *There's a right person for you out there somewhere.* There may very well be. The myth is that once you find the right person, everything will be all right. My hunch is you're smart enough to know why that's a myth. The current divorce rate pretty much says it all.[1] Consider this. Every man and woman who have navigated the pain and complexity of divorce stood in front of a preacher, priest, or justice of the peace and made vows to the *right* person. Every single one. But eventually they discovered something wrong with Mr. or Miss Right. Then there's this. A good many divorced men and women had already located right person 2.0 while in the process of divorcing right person 1.0. And the whole thing begins again.

You may not believe there's *one* right person for you, but you are looking for the *right* person. Aren't you? Of course you are. What option do you have? Go looking for the wrong person? No person? How 'bout an arranged marriage?

There's a thought. Who would your parents have *arranged* for you?

Looking for the right person is a great idea as long as you don't assume that finding the right person ensures everything will be all right. Looking for the right person is essential; it's just not enough. There's more to a satisfying relationship than finding the right person. As I mentioned in the introduction, *more* is what this book is all about. Problem is, we don't hear much about the *more* side of the relational equation. Understandably so. It doesn't make for great film or reality TV. However, it does make for great relationships. It's this undervalued side of the equation that keeps romance romantic. On a personal note, it's why I love going home at the end of the day. TMI.

Attraction Matters

Before we explore *more*, let's think together for just a paragraph or two about what makes a *right* person a *right* person. There are a number of factors, among them beauty, talent, confidence, intelligence, depth, wit, family, wealth, weight, height, career, and personality. Admit it, you have a list. Everybody has a list. Online dating services wouldn't work if people didn't have lists. But at the end of the day, our lists are not the deciding factors, are they? In the end it comes down to two things (actually maybe one thing, but for the sake of clarity I'll keep them separate): chemistry and attraction. At age fifteen, attraction is enough. But I doubt there are too many fifteen-year-olds reading this. While most everybody has a mental list of what makes the *right person* the *right person*, most people abandon their lists for physical attraction and chemistry.

When you're physically attracted to someone *and* there's that extra something we will refer to as chemistry, it just feels right, doesn't it?

When it feels right, it's easy to assume it *is* right. And sometimes it is.

This explains why we've heard people say, "The first time we met, I knew we would be together." Somehow they just knew. They *knew* before they got to *know* each other. Strange. Strange but not uncommon. While instant chemistry is common, instant chemistry that dovetails into an instantly healthy relationship with until-death-do-us-part potential is not. Show me a couple who are attracted to each other and share that certain something, and I'll show you a couple convinced they are *right* for each other. So *right* that nothing could possibly go *wrong*. Right? Been there? We all have. But as I'm fond of saying, falling in love is easy; it requires a pulse. Staying in love requires *more*. There's that word again.

Since the title of this book promises SEX, I thought we should introduce the topic in this first chapter. But this isn't the sex talk. That's in chapter eight. If you can't wait, feel free to flip or swipe ahead ... as long as you promise to come back and read the first seven chapters.

When a relationship feels *right*, it's a powerful thing. Deceptively powerful. It's no wonder that the *righter* a relationship feels, the *quicker* we are tempted to take things further. Why not? Physical attraction isn't like art appreciation. It's not something you admire from a distance. Physical attraction is like hunger. It's something you satisfy. It's part of the attraction–chemistry continuum. If a couple shares a passion for the same foods, music, and sports teams, it makes sense they need to find out if that passion extends to the bedroom. And what do you know? In the majority of cases, it does. While adding a dose of physical involvement into the mix makes a relationship more exciting and enjoyable, it also makes it more complicated. But for the most part, that doesn't stop us, which brings us to our first "doesn't everybody know that?" moment. This is where I state the obvious, with a preposition at the end.

Ready?

You are sexually compatible with far more people than you are relationally compatible with.

Not a single male reading this book will underline that statement. Of course our sexual compatibility outstrips our relational compatibility. By a long shot. Several million to one. Which means if you're sexually involved with someone right now, the next time the two of you are in the middle of lovemaking, look each other in the eye and say, "You are one *of* a million!" To which your partner will say (assuming he or she hasn't read this fascinating book), "Don't you mean, I'm one *in* a million?" To which you can say, "No, you're one *of* a million. I'm sexually compatible with a million other people. You're just one of 'em!"

Okay. Terrible idea.

This "tell me something I don't already know" insight underscores why experimenting sexually to ensure you've found the *right person* is a bad idea. Sexual compatibility is important. Real important. But sexual compatibility is not the litmus test for relational compatibility. In fact, it's the other way around. Exhibit A: Why did your last relationship end? What happened? Did it have anything to do with sexual incompatibility? Losing interest in sex with someone isn't the same as being sexually incompatible. Losing interest in sex with someone is always a manifestation of something else. Something deeper. My hunch is the root of your previous relational challenges was ... relational, not sexual. Chances are you would have addressed the relational challenges more quickly if you hadn't been physically involved. In fact, you would have ended the relationship sooner if you hadn't been sexually involved. Sex is a bit like glue. You shouldn't apply it until you're absolutely sure you're ready to stick two things together permanently. Apply it too soon, and you'll have a mess once you realize your mistake. I know, sounds like something your momma would say.

Not only is sex not the litmus test for relational compatibility, it actually inhibits and distracts from relational development. Why? Because sex has the capacity to camouflage an endless list of relational deficiencies and dysfunctions. Romance overpowers objectivity, which will work to your advantage in marriage. But before marriage, a lack of objectivity is dangerous. Sex distorts positive and negative traits in a partner. Men and women exaggerate the good and turn a blind eye to the things that would normally give them pause. Once a couple is physically involved, they overlook and ignore characteristics and habits that would otherwise cause them to mark someone off their lists.

Now, if you can relate to the previous three paragraphs and you're wondering why you weren't smart enough to recognize what was happening when it was happening, I have a bit of encouraging news. It wasn't completely your fault. Your brain played a trick on you. For years researchers have studied the brain's response to a variety of external stimuli, including specific appetites.

Along the way they discovered a cognitive bias someone labeled *focalism*. Focalism is the brain's tendency to magnify one thing to the exclusion of everything else. Focalism distorts reality, be that reality food, a dress, a car, or, yes, a person. You've experienced focalism many times, and most instances were harmless. We've all driven miles out of our way to get a favorite dessert, fast food sandwich, or specialty coffee. We had to have *that* particular one. Nothing else would suffice. We've all made impulse purchases we later regretted. Similarly, we've tried our best to buy something, attend something, or contact someone that didn't work out. Twenty-four hours later, we were relieved that it didn't. Focalism, along with a short list of other cognitive biases, has the potential to trick us into making bad decisions. That potential increases dramatically in emotionally charged environments. And what's more emotionally charged than romance?

Romance is like a fog. Nobody sees clearly. Couples begin to believe no one has *ever* loved the way they love. Not their mommas or their grandmommas. Not Romeo and Juliet. Not William and Kate. Not even Edward and Bella.

It's almost impossible to recognize any of this in the mirror. But you immediately recognize it in your friends, don't you? You've had friends introduce you to Mr. or Miss Right, and you thought, *Seriously? Really? Have you lost your mind?* They're thinking happily ever after and you're wondering if it's too late to say something. You know intuitively that they're as happy as they'll ever be. Once the sizzle subsides, somebody is going to wake up and wonder how he or she got into this mess. And you're not the only one who's noticed. Everybody sees it. Everybody but them.

Doesn't Make Him Right

The odds are in your favor. You will be sexually compatible with the *right* person. But sexual compatibility doesn't make someone *right*. If it did, things would sure be easier. That arranged marriage approach would work just about 100 percent of the time. Sex is easy. Relationships are not. To test the potential possibility of a long-term relationship via sex is a bit like choosing a university because it looks like a university. Most universities look like universities.

If you allow attraction and chemistry to sweep you immediately into sexual involvement, you will most likely confuse sexual compatibility for something it isn't. Namely, a sign. The fact that you can't keep your hands off of her ... the fact that you can't wait for him to get his hands on you ... is not a sign of anything other than you are two healthy people who have stumbled across one of the many other healthy people in the world with whom you are sexually compatible. Makes you wonder if this *right person* phenomenon is nature's way of ensuring the human race survives even if relationships don't.

Slow Fade

Physical attraction and chemistry combined with a routine of "my house or yours?" has the potential to diminish the importance of what you've always believed was important for a healthy, go-the-distance relationship. We've never met. But I bet we would agree on what it takes to create a relationship that stands the test of time and the unavoidable trials of life. Unfortunately, those very things get lost or downgraded in the bliss of "we're the exception to all the rules" passion. Treating what's important as unimportant has a price tag. A big price tag. Perhaps you've already paid that tab a time or two. Perhaps it's why you capitulated and bought a book about something you always assumed you could figure out on your own. If that's the case, bear with me as I address my readers who have yet to find themselves in a relationship that promised much but delivered little.

As I mentioned earlier, falling in love requires only a pulse. Staying in love requires *more*. When a couple ignores *more*, they have relationship problems. Why? Because in the beginning they ignored all of that silly relationship stuff. They didn't need it. That was for other people, people who weren't in love like they were in love. But, over time, the connection that was once so effortless and passionate, so sexually charged, begins to fade. Instead of chemistry and passion, there's tension and frustration. The chemistry that fueled the *right person* mystique ebbs. Both parties begin looking for ways to return things to their former state. Guys suggest more sex. After all, that's what fueled things in the beginning. Guys view sex like a wrench. More on that later. Women are generally the first to use the "R" word. "I think we need to talk about our relationship." Women are often the first to recommend outside help. Men generally don't want any help. With anything. I'll tell you why. The way we figure it, we didn't need any outside help in the beginning, so why would we need it now? We didn't need a counselor to help us fall in love. We shouldn't have to hire a counselor to keep us in love. Besides, counseling is just a bunch of words. Like this book. So we don't go. And we don't buy relationship books.

Dumb Married Tricks

As attraction and chemistry wane, it's not uncommon for somebody to suggest having a baby. Men think, *Well, that requires sex, so yeah.* If you've never been married, you're thinking, *Why would anyone bring a baby into a relationship that's already on life support?* Good question. If you're married, or were married, you may be wondering why you didn't ask yourself that very question. But don't beat yourself up. You were looking for a way back. A way back to what you had. To what you felt. You were looking for common ground. Common interest. Couples try all kinds of things to rekindle what once was. As they should. The alternatives aren't good. Give up or soldier on in a lifeless, passionless relationship. My point is, finding the *right person* is no guarantee that things will turn out *right*. In fact, leaning into the right person myth almost guarantees they won't.

All the Wrong Options

Before we move on, I want to go back to the "maybe a baby will help" idea. Bringing a baby into a troubled relationship is a bad idea for many reasons. Not least of which is that one of the most morally vulnerable times in the life of a man is when his wife or girlfriend is pregnant. This is true in healthy relationships, but the temptation is compounded when things aren't going well. While 15 percent of married couples divorce within three years of the birth of their first child,[2] the percentage of unmarried couples who separate after the birth of a child is closer to 40 percent.[3] Children aren't a solution. They aren't meant to be. Children should be a welcomed addition to a healthy family unit.

But men aren't the only ones who start looking elsewhere when things aren't going well. As the *right person* approach starts unraveling, everybody is open to a new *right person*. And social media has made it easier than ever to wade through the options.

In fact, second marriages have a higher failure rate than first marriages. Sixty-seven percent of second and 73 percent of third marriages end in divorce. Know why? People approach a second marriage the way they did their first one. They go looking for the next right person. Why not? Once you find the *right person*, everything will be all right.

Right?

Anyone?

Mirror, Mirror

So if *finding* the right person doesn't guarantee everything will be all right, what does?

Nothing.

Nothing *guarantees* everything will be all right. But there *is* an approach that will increase your odds. Significantly. In chapter two I'll start unpacking it for you. But before we go there, I need you to do me a big favor. If you're currently in a relationship your friends and your momma disapprove of— and you and Mr. or Miss Right seem to be the only ones who are certain the relationship is *right*—slow down. A lot. Better yet, would you hit the pause button until you've finished this book? Please. What you feel is real. But it may not be reliable. I've never met a happy couple whose story included, "Everybody, including our parents, told us we had no business being together, but we ignored their advice and we're glad we did." On the other hand, I've talked to dozens of people whose relationships ended poorly and who admitted they were warned but refused to listen. They believed love (or whatever it was) was enough. But it wasn't. It never is. Many of those folks admitted they had reservations. But out of stubbornness, or a desire to prove somebody wrong, or fear of regret because of moral boundaries they had crossed, they pushed ahead. They tuned out the voices of those who loved them most and made the biggest mistake of their lives. It felt *right* at the time. Of course it did. They'd found the *right* person. So, do me a favor. Hit the pause button. You'll be glad you did.

CHAPTER 2

COMMITMENT IS OVERRATED

Every Saturday, in cities all over America, starry-eyed couples join hands, say vows, exchange rings, and make promises they have every *intention* of keeping but with little to no *preparation* for doing so. They mean well. I doubt there are many instances of brides or grooms being intentionally dishonest. But in the majority of cases these well-intentioned, beautifully adorned men and women make promises they just aren't equipped to keep.

Chances are you've attended a wedding where you suspected this to be the case. You wished the couple well, but in your heart you suspected things weren't going to go well. You've witnessed couples making commitments you suspected they weren't prepared to keep. You didn't need a crystal ball to predict their future or a bookie to determine their odds. You wished 'em the best but saved your receipt. The tension you experienced in that intuitive moment was based on your suspicion that they weren't prepared for what they promised.

In the realm of relationships, unlike any other arena of life, we operate from the premise that a *promise* replaces the need for *preparation*. That a couple can *promise*, *vow*, or *commit* themselves into a successful future. But our experience in other areas proves that to be patently false. In the world of academics, sports, business, medicine — you name the field — preparation is the key to success. There's not a college coach anywhere who would dream of substituting promises or vows for preparation. Coaches know that you don't promise to win games; you prepare to win. Good students know they must prepare for exams, not just stare in the mirror and promise to do well. It's one thing to sign up for a race; it's another thing to prepare for it. If you're not prepared, it's a waste of time to promise a good finish time. In every arena of life, preparation is the key to success. This is true for relationships as well.

But for reasons having more to do with marketing than common sense, our culture completely ignores this indisputable reality. Very few people *prepare*. Most people are content to *commit*. When it comes to relationships, commitment is way overrated. WAY. Promises and commitments are no substitute for preparation.

Capable vs. Accountable

Saying "I do" doesn't make a person *capable*, only *accountable*. When you're *accountable* for something you're not *capable* of, you will eventually be *miserable*. Remember Algebra 2? Was it just me? If you marry or commit yourself to someone who is not prepared to reciprocate, you're going to hold the person accountable. Which means you are going to make his or her life *miserable*. And his or her lack of commitment will become the primary source of your own misery. Sounds pretty miserable.

Again, you can't promise, commit, or vow your way past a lack of preparation. Neither can the person you are promising, committing, or vowing to. A promise is no substitute for preparation. You must prepare to commit if your commitment is going to mean anything. And your partner must as well.

So do yourself a big favor. Don't make a relational commitment you aren't prepared to keep. Notice I didn't say *committed* to keep. Prepared to keep. And don't commit yourself to someone who is unprepared to keep his or her commitment to you. Odds are you've already done that somewhere along the way. You don't want a repeat performance. But in order to avoid one, you must begin thinking and behaving differently.

Which brings us to the important but extraordinarily uncomfortable question: *How do you know?* How do you know if you're prepared to commit? How do you know if your *right person* is prepared?

Everybody Ought to Know

Fortunately, the answer to that question is simple. Unfortunately, it's so simple nobody pays much attention to it.

Well, almost nobody. Parents do. The best way to know if someone is prepared to commit is to examine his or her prior commitments. If you want to know how someone will behave tomorrow, take a look at what he or she did yesterday.

Are there exceptions?

Of course.

Should you make a significant relationship decision assuming you will be the exception?

Never.

As in never ever.

It's too risky. Not only that, it's unnecessary.

Every couple thinks they are the exception. Chalk that up to chemistry and romance. The good news is, there are ways to discover whether you might be the exception without gambling with your relational future.

Don't Take My Word for It

The notion of an inexorable link between preparation and the ability to keep a promise is certainly not original with me. Neither is the connection between past and future performance. Oddly enough, the embryo of both ideas is found in a statement made thousands of years ago by one of the wisest men who ever lived, King Solomon. In his library of proverbs we find the following:

> The simple believe anything, but the prudent give thought to their steps.
>
> (PROVERBS 14:15)

"The simple believe anything." The term translated *simple* is also translated *naïve* in other ancient Hebrew literature. Naïve people are those who believe just about anything they are told. Being naïve is not an IQ problem; it stems from a lack of experience. This is why we associate the term with younger people. Time and life have a way of erasing naiveté. Only a naïve person would think to run a marathon without training. And only a naïve couple would enter a marriage based on a promise alone, even if they exchanged rings as part of their commitment. Their lack of preparation in the days leading up to the marriage would be a good predictor of their performance after the wedding day. Wouldn't it?

And now for the second part of Solomon's couplet:

... but the prudent give thought to their steps.

We don't talk about *prudent* people much these days. A prudent person is someone who understands life is connected, that today's decisions have implications for tomorrow's reality. Prudent people understand that what we do today is a good indication of how we will behave tomorrow. While naïve people tend to view events and decisions in *isolation*, the prudent person assumes a *connection*. The prudent person knows the best indicator of her future behavior is her past behavior.

The term *steps* in this proverb refers to direction. You know the future direction of a thing by connecting the dots of where said thing has been. The future is always potential. The past is measurable and observable. The past makes the future predictable.

Solomon's point? Prudent people, wise men and women, put very little stock in promises. Instead, they look carefully at the trajectory of their lives and the lives of those around them. If you want to know where you're headed, all you have to do is look back to see where you've been. If you want to know where your *right person* is headed, just take a look at where he or she has been. Discount the promises but pay attention to the dots, the patterns. Again, the paths people choose trump the commitments they make. The paths people have chosen trump the promises they've made. *The past is a better indicator than a promise.*

Sound a bit harsh?

Ungraceful?

Unforgiving?

Is there a voice in your head screaming, "But people change!" or, "But she's trying," or, "He's doing better"? What about, "He has a job interview tomorrow"? "She hasn't had a drink in two weeks"? "He hasn't missed a single visit with his parole officer"?

I understand. I really do. I'm all for forgiveness and grace. And I believe that people change. But I don't believe that *people* change *people*. And I don't believe that people change *for* people. People change themselves. People change themselves when they get sick and tired of themselves, when the pain of staying the same is too great to bear or there's a goal so enticing that it draws them away from what and who they used to be.

But no one *depends* his or her way to change. People *depend* their way into dependency. Dependency leads to a loss of self-respect, which often leads to a loss of respect from the person the dependent person is depending upon. And that usually leads to a loss of relationship.

My point? If you are in a relationship with someone who has a spotty track record relationally, financially, professionally, morally, chemical dependently ... and this special person is promising that the future will be different now that *you* are in his life, please pay careful attention to the next couple of paragraphs. And no, you aren't going to like them. And yes, somebody else has probably already told you this. And no, I have not been talking to your momma.

Think for a minute about the biggest positive change you've made in your life thus far: relational, financial, professional, academic, whatever. It may have involved breaking a habit or addiction. What is something you are proud of having accomplished because it represents a major stride forward for you?

Next, think about your greatest regret. Not something that happened *to* you, but a regret that involved a decision or series of decisions *you* made. A regret that you brought in part upon yourself. Got it? Now be honest. What was the primary contributor to the event or season of your life you regret most? Chances are someone else was involved. Perhaps a group of people. People you liked. People you trusted. Our greatest regrets often do. It may have been someone you loved. You believed moving in his or her direction would make your life better, richer. But in the end, it wasn't so.

Now reflect on the change that has made the greatest positive impact on your life to date. It may have been the decision to leave the individual or individuals associated with your greatest regret. Perhaps it was a decision to go to school or go back to school. You may have broken an addiction or attempted something that drew you out of your comfort zone.

Last question: What contributed most to that positive change? You may have been encouraged by others. You may have found inspiration in the stories of others. Perhaps someone you respected and loved believed in you and spoke to your potential. But in the end, wasn't it *your* decision to act, to engage, to move forward, to move out, that brought about the change you celebrate? You did not *depend* your way forward. On the contrary, you in-depended your way forward. You came to the point where you knew you had to change, and you decided that no matter what it took, things were going to be different. You made up your mind that the status quo was no more. And once you did, you fought your way through. You shook something off. You moved on with your life. You *chose* your way forward. Others may have cheered you on. But the change came about because of something *you* did for *you*.

Right?

Here's my point: Nobody changed you. You changed you. If you're religious, you may say God changed you or God helped you to change. But when all was said and done, the change that occurred took place because you made up your mind to change.

So please hear me. If you're in a relationship with someone who is depending on you to help him or her become a better person (i.e., change), it's not going to happen. That is beyond your ability. You can't change another person for the better any more than that person can change you. *People will change when they decide to change.* If you're in a relationship because you believe your *right person* is going to help you change, you're wasting your most valuable resource: time. To put it bluntly, you're wasting your life. Your *right person* can't change you. You are expecting the impossible. In fact, the dependency you have developed is probably an impediment to the change you long to experience. *You will change when you decide to change.* Again, no one depends his or her way to change. Change requires fierce in-dependence that should eventually lead to inter-dependence with other healthy people.

With that in mind, I would like to make a suggestion. If you have concerns about the direction in which your *right person* is moving in life, give her time and space to change. I know; I know; you love her. All the more reason to give her time and space to get her life together. Time and space equals respect. Time and space says, "I know you can do this, and you don't need me as a crutch."

And yes, if you give her time and space, you may lose her. She may go in search of another crutch. Somebody else to depend on. You may cry yourself to sleep or drink yourself into a stupor. Either way, you're better off. Because, as it turns out, she wasn't the *right person* for you after all. She's not in a position to keep the promise she's made or is planning to make. She's not prepared to commit. If she needs you to help her become someone who can keep her promise, where does that leave you? So give her time and space.

Speeding in the Wrong Direction

I've never met a couple that wished they had moved faster. I have talked to hundreds of fresh-out-of-a-relationship individuals who wished they had moved slower. I've talked to more people than I can count who went into relationships with the goal of *helping* or *changing* their partner. Perhaps you've already tried that. Perhaps you were on the other side of the equation. You latched onto someone you believed could help you. And he did. For a while. Until you wore him out and now he's moved on to help someone else. And you aren't feeling very "helped." You are no better off than when you met him. Just older. Perhaps bitter. If that's the case, keep reading. I'm not going to leave you hanging.

So yes, people change. They change direction; they get healthier; they break habits, overcome addictions. But until they do, they will be unable to keep their promises and follow through on their vows. If you believe the change your *right person* is promising depends on you, you are making a gamble that in all probability will not pay off. Might as well drive around with your seatbelt unbuckled. Every once in a while, people walk away from collisions that occurred when they were not wearing their seatbelts. It's possible. But I'm guessing you'll continue to buckle up. Sure wish you would consider that same approach in the arena of romance. Seatbelts are a hassle. Waiting for someone to change before jumping into a relationship is a hassle. But both are worth the hassle. Seatbelts save lives. Sitting on the sidelines while someone you care about gets his life together may save you a chapter or two of unnecessary regret.

When you hear (or hear yourself saying) any of the following lines, you owe it to yourself to press pause:

- "I can't live without you."
- "I can't make it without you."
- "I'm not sure I want to live without you."
- "I'll never overcome this without you."
- "With your help, I can become a better person."
- "Before you came along, I was lost."
- "I need you."
- "I'm incomplete without you."

On the silver screen or in your favorite romance novel those lines usually lead to good things. But in the real world they lead to hard times. They are red flags. Those are *declarations of dependence*. They're tantamount to saying, "I'm weak; you're strong. I need you to be strong for both of us." For some personalities, that's an irresistible invitation. Caretakers love to provide care. Fixers love to fix. Rescuers love to rescue. You may be among that special group who has never seen a need you didn't want to meet. Especially when the "need" is hot or rich. But none of that changes the fact that you cannot fix other people. You cannot change them. You can prop them up until you are worn out. In the end, they will be who they are—and you will be tired.

If you *really* care, create space and wait. If the other person really cares, he or she won't fault you for your decision. What's the rush? What are you afraid of?

Don't be *simple*.

Give thought to the other person's *steps*.

Don't be *simple*.

Give thought to your *steps*.

Commit. Not to a person, not to a relationship. Commit *now* to preparing to keep your commitments *later*. That's the goal, what you should focus on. If you do, when you say "I do," you'll be prepared to follow through. If all this leaves you wondering how one prepares to make commitments he or she is prepared to keep, keep reading.

CHAPTER 3

BECOMING THE RIGHT PERSON

S o far we've established two things. First, finding the *right person* doesn't ensure everything will be *all right*. Second, committing to something we haven't prepared for is a recipe for failure in any arena, relationships included. So there's *more* to happiness than finding someone and saying the right things. From this point we are going to explore *more*. But in case you're one of those people who starts more books than you finish, I'll go ahead and sum it up for you: Become the *right* person. *Becoming* the right person is how you prepare to commit. *Becoming* the right person dramatically increases your odds of sustained relational success when you finally *meet* the right person. As we are about to discover, becoming the right person dramatically increases the likelihood of being *attracted* to the person who is *right* for you. If you are as intentional about *becoming* the right person as you are about *meeting* the right person, you will position yourself to bypass a boatload of unnecessary pain, regret, and wasted time. I'm absolutely convinced people who are committed to becoming the right people are better equipped to identify and avoid the wrong people along the way.

Makes sense when you think about it. This, of course, is the problem. We don't think about it. Athletes don't look for the *right team* before becoming the type of player the *right team* is looking for. You didn't apply to the *right school* before working to become the person the *right school* was looking for. In the marketplace we call this résumé building. We know intuitively that we are responsible for what we bring to the table in every arena of life. We know that to be worth hiring, interning, or receiving a scholarship, we have to become someone worth hiring, interning, or receiving a scholarship. Relationships are no different.

A Girl Like You

While conducting a focus group on this topic, a young lady shared an incident from her life that left everyone in the group speechless. It illustrates the importance of *becoming* the right person in a most unforgettable way. Denise grew up in a religious home. When she graduated from college, she moved to Atlanta and immersed herself in our dating culture. Her words: "You know, it's not that I quit believing what I used to believe; it's just that I kind of took all of that and I just put it on the back burner for a season. I decided when it came to dating and my relationship with guys, I wasn't going to factor God into the mix."

Before long, her lifestyle bore little trace of the religious values and morals she had been raised to embrace. Dating was just another form of entertainment. Guys came. Guys went. There was guilt. But there were ways to deal with guilt. She wasn't doing anything that everybody around her wasn't doing. There weren't any significant consequences. She even prayed occasionally. Life was actually pretty good. She developed some effective coping skills for those times when life wasn't so good.

Then she met the *right* person.

It happened at a friend's apartment complex during a party. An hour or so into the evening, a guy she'd never seen before walked in, and she knew immediately that he was somebody she needed to meet. Before the night was over, she managed to get herself introduced to Mitchel and his group of friends. In her words, he was "the total package" — looks, personality, career, everything. A few minutes into the conversation it became apparent Mitchel was a Christian. And in a lifestyle sense, not just a cultural one. He was serious about his faith. Even in a social setting it was evident that faith was integral to every aspect of his life. Denise found this strangely appealing. It surfaced those things she had put in a box for later. Denise left the party determined to find a way to cross paths with Mitchel again.

The following weekend Denise drove home to visit her family. On Saturday afternoon she was talking with her mom while folding clothes. It wasn't long before her encounter with Mitchel surfaced. She went on and on about his looks, his job, his maturity. Before she realized it, she began talking about his faith. Specifically about how central it was to his life and lifestyle. "Mom," she said, "he's like a real Christian. He's the kind of guy I've been looking for." Denise said it was at that point in the conversation that her mom put down what she was doing, looked up at Denise, and said, "Sweetheart, the problem is, a guy like that is not looking for a girl like you."

Denise said she literally fell to the floor in a puddle of tears and cried and cried and cried. Her mom was right. There was no denying it. This was a defining moment for Denise as a single woman. In a flash, the values, beliefs, and childhood faith she had put on the back burner flooded her soul. She was overwhelmed with who she had allowed herself to become. So, in that moment, she decided to become the type of person the person she was looking for was looking for. In that moment, she decided to change everything that wasn't aligned with who she wanted to be. By her own admission, there was a lot that needed changing: priorities, values, friendships, where she would and wouldn't go, and who she would and wouldn't go with.

Denise's story brings us to *the* question I hope to stick in the epicenter of your thinking for as long as you're single: *Are you the person the person you're looking for is looking for?* If not, like Denise, are you willing to begin the process of *becoming* the person the person you're looking for is looking for? If you made a list of what you are looking for in someone (which isn't a bad idea), would that person be looking for someone like you? If the other person's list matched your list, how would you measure up? If your *right person* is the sum of the things on your list, what do you suppose his or her list looks like? You? Now, is it just me, or is there something a bit hypocritical about wanting something in someone else that you've not been willing to develop in yourself?

Do you hate me yet?

Bottom line, it's not enough to look; you must become. You must become intentional about becoming the person the person you're looking for is looking for.

Nobody Does This

Now, before I lose you, let me go ahead and state what somebody out there is thinking: *Andy, nobody thinks this way. Nobody is preparing to commit. Why should I be the first?* Whenever I teach this material, someone will track me down afterward and express that exact sentiment. When I hear it, I always respond the same way: "I think what you meant to say is, 'You don't *know* anybody who thinks this way. You don't know anyone who is preparing to commit.'"

I've been talking about this long enough to know that you may not believe what I'm about to tell you. But it's absolutely true. *If you commit to prepare before you promise, it will dramatically increase your chances of crossing paths with someone who is preparing as well.* Why? Because *preparing* for anything sensitizes you to people who share your passion and direction. Preparation forces you to focus your time; it means saying no to some opportunities while saying yes to others. If you choose to prepare yourself relationally, you will gravitate toward environments that aid you in that pursuit.

In the same way, it will bring you into contact with those who share your priorities.

When people complain that "nobody" thinks this way, what they're really saying is, "The people I work with, live with, and socialize with don't think this way." Which means they may need to reevaluate the folks with whom they *work, live, and socialize*. Perhaps you do as well. But before you shut me off too quickly, remember this: *you rarely make eye contact with drivers moving in the opposite direction.*

That was helpful, wasn't it?

Think for a minute. Who do you glance over and make eye contact with when you're speeding down the highway at sixty-five-plus miles an hour? People across the median or those moving in the same direction?

Okay, maybe a different car analogy will help.

Ever bought a new car? Or maybe a new-to-you car? Do you remember thinking how odd it was that so many other people ran out and purchased the same brand and make of automobile? Your car was everywhere. You had no idea you were such a trendsetter. Actually, you began noticing something that had been there all along. You just hadn't noticed it before. Don't ever forget: We *see* what we're *looking* for. We see *whom* we're looking for as well. Truth is, there are plenty of single people who are preparing to make relational commitments they can keep. But until your life is moving in that direction, you may never make eye contact. You may never notice them. But I assure you, they're out there.

Rarely a week goes by that I don't run into a couple who met in one of our Atlanta-area churches. I always ask the same question: "How did you meet?" In the majority of cases they met while serving on one of our volunteer teams. Either out in our community, or on one of our church campuses, or on one of the overseas trips we sponsor every year. They were engaged in something productive—an others-centered activity—and what do you know, they met somebody cute who shared their interest and passion to do for others. As my wife's mother told her growing up, "If you go to the right places, chances are you will meet the right people." For the record, Sandra and I met at a Bible study on the campus of Georgia Tech.

Figures.

Don't get nervous. I don't believe church people are the only ones preparing to commit. Church happens to be my context. Online dating services provide a similar context. While plenty of nightmare stories are associated with online dating, the success rate speaks for itself. Happily married couples who met online have something in common. They learned to read between the lines of online profiles to determine the direction in which a potential match was headed. Personal interests and hobbies are interesting. Direction is determinative.

Jenny and Shane are great examples. I've known Jenny for over twenty years. Jenny was that single lady who everyone was always shocked to discover had always been single. Talented, attractive, outgoing, made her own clothes. Okay, I'm making up the last part. Sandra and I lost touch with Jenny for a few years, and then suddenly she showed back up via social media, married with teenage kids. So we invited her and Shane, whom we had never met, to breakfast to get the scoop. Shane's wife had died four years earlier after a long battle with cancer. A year later, he entered the fascinating and confusing world of online dating. He learned quickly that his age (early fifties) and business success made him a commodity. He commented, "The whole thing was shocking to me. The first three women I met assumed I was interested primarily in sex, and they were more than willing to oblige." Actually, that's not exactly what he said; I cleaned it up a bit. "After my third date I went back and rewrote my profile to better reflect my values and morals, which I thought were pretty clear the first time, but apparently not!" he added. Meanwhile, Jenny had run across Shane's profile and was intrigued. But she'd been in and out of the world of online dating for several years and had her own list of bad date experiences. While Shane's original profile made him sound "moralish" and an all-around "good guy," she'd seen plenty of those before. So she passed. Once he posted his upgraded version, she decided to take a chance. When I say *upgraded*, I mean he spelled it out. He smiled and said, "It was so strong, I assumed I had sealed my fate in cyber world. When my daughter read it, she said, 'Dad, no normal woman is going to be interested in you.'" To which Jenny interrupted and said, "And she was right. But I was!" We all laughed. Several weeks later, they met for coffee. Isn't that always how it begins, coffee? Jenny showed up with two friends in case she needed rescuing. As it turns out, she didn't. Funny thing about Jenny and Shane, they really don't have much in common on paper. Their common ground, as is so often the case with successful relationships, was more directional than recreational. Their lives were moving in a common direction. Their common direction quickly blossomed into mutual affection.

I should have been a poet.

Regardless

Regardless of your context or worldview, becoming the person the person you are looking for is looking for greatly increases your odds of finding someone doing the same thing. Someone who is merely looking for the *right person* usually winds up with someone merely looking for the *right person*. But people committed to *becoming* the right people are usually attracted to and notice individuals who are doing the same. Like attracts like. Again, we see what and whom we are looking for. So, perhaps it's time to adjust your orientation. No, not that one. Your *right person* orientation. Instead of being so focused on *looking*, perhaps you should commit a bit more energy to *becoming*. Don't give up on your quest to fall in love with someone who has prepared to love you in return. It still happens. It can happen for you. But it probably won't happen until you let go of the right person myth and determine instead to focus your attention on *becoming the person the person you are looking for is looking for*. Prepare to commit so that when the day of commitment arrives, you will, in fact, be prepared. As we will discover in the next chapter, this is what you were created for. I don't want you to miss it. You don't want to miss it either.

CHAPTER 4

SO BECOMING

There are scores of books designed to help couples build or rebuild a healthy relationship. This is not one of those books. This is a book written to help *you* build a better *you* so that *you* will be equipped to build a better relationship. The healthier you are, the healthier your relationships will be. Truth is, your relationships will never be any healthier than you. Here's why.

And this is important.

Relationships are never stronger than the weakest link. Granted, *link* is a bit harsh. But I think you know what I mean. The stronger, more mature, more secure person in a relationship is always forced to make up for, defer to, or fill in the gaps created by the weaker person. If you grew up with a brother or sister who created chaos in your home due to bad habits or unhealthy lifestyle choices, you know what I'm talking about. That sibling got the lion's share of attention while you, the straight-A student who stayed out of trouble, got whatever was left over. Your parents spent far more time talking about, worrying about, and praying about the wild child than the other children in your family combined. The entire family dynamic was impacted and possibly dictated by the weakest link.

The same is true for couples. If you're the weak link, your relationship will never be any healthier than you. If your partner is the weak link, the relationship will never be healthier than your partner. That's why I say, the relationship won't get any *better* than you. So, the better you become, the happier everybody will be. And if you determine to wait until you find someone who is committed to becoming a better version of him- or herself, well, everybody wins. As I stated in the introduction, couples generally don't have *relationship* problems. They have problems they bring to the relationship. The better *you* that you bring, the fewer problems you bring with *you*. And of course the same is true of your future partner.

Once Upon a Time

When it comes to becoming the best possible version of you, I'm convinced the best place to begin is with the Beginner. If you're like most people, you fall into the theological category of *theist*—that is, you believe in a God. Chances are you believe your God of choice had something to do with the creation of the world. Either directly or indirectly, you probably believe God is responsible for creating you. But here's something you may not have considered. The ability for humanity to experience, develop, and maintain *relationship* is in itself a creation. Once upon a time, or perhaps before time, relationship didn't exist. If, like me, you believe in a personal God, then it's not difficult to accept that the ability to pursue, initiate, and sustain a satisfying relationship is a *gift* God gave to the human race. It's impossible to imagine life without relationships. Having personally experienced the satisfaction of long-term friendships, a twenty-something-year marriage, and the joy of being a father, I know my life would not be nearly as rich without relationships. In addition to relationship, God also created sex. Think about that for a moment. Only a moment. Once upon a time, there was no sex. God thought it up. Next time you're asked to say the blessing before Thanksgiving dinner, throw that into the mix of things you're grateful for. If nothing else, it will pretty much ensure you won't be tasked with that responsibility again.

If God created and gave us the capacity for satisfying relationships, it's reasonable to assume God knows a thing or two about how to prepare for and operate one. Ever purchase something from a big box retailer and open the box to find a card that reads something along these lines? *If this product is defective or a piece is missing, do not return to the place of purchase. Instead, contact us at 1-800-ITS-YOUR FAULT.* The reason the manufacturer would prefer you call them first is because they are the manufacturer. They know more than the retailer about their product. Way more. They also know operator error is more likely to blame than a manufacturing defect. So they would prefer that you *call* before you *return.* Relationally speaking, when a relationship isn't working properly, it's tempting to go stand in the return line rather than check with the manufacturer. That's unfortunate. It explains why relational history has a way of repeating itself.

Instructions

In addition to creating our capacity for relationship, God has given us instruction in how best to conduct our relationships. The core essentials for relational health are clearly explained in the second half of the Bible, the New Testament. In fact, the New Testament contains the single most powerful relational principle known to man. A single idea, that when applied, resolves all relational conflict immediately. That's right. Immediately. I know; that's a big promise. But it's true. Speaking of promises, I promise to fill you in on the details later in this chapter.

As you may know, the New Testament is a collection of texts written primarily as a way to introduce post–first-century generations to the person, works, and words of Jesus. More to the point of our discussion, the New Testament provides us with the foundational behaviors and perspectives necessary for satisfying and enduring relationships. Embracing the teaching of the New Testament will prepare you to commit.

But there's a catch.

Against the Grain

The New Testament can be compared to an unsanded board. Run your hand in the direction of the grain, and it's smooth. Run your hand against the grain, and you may come away with splinters. In a similar fashion, if you approach the New Testament asking, "How do I *find* the right person?" the text is silent. But once you muster the courage to ask, "How do I *become* the right person?" the text comes alive. Similarly, come to the New Testament asking, "How do I change my partner?" Crickets. But ask, "How do I change myself?" Splinters. So in this chapter we're going to open the New Testament and ask the relational questions these ancient and sacred texts were written to answer.

In the first century there was no "singles culture" to speak of. Nobody dated. Come to think of it, nobody really *dates* nowadays either. Well, almost nobody. I hear a lot of married couples talk about scheduling a "date night." I don't think my parents scheduled "date nights." Not sure when that started. I got married so I could quit dating.

Anyway.

In the first century there was no dating. Parents arranged their children's marriages. You may remember that from the Christmas story. I've often wondered who my parents would have *betrothed* me to marry. It's not a question many of us want to spend too much time thinking about.

While the New Testament says nothing of dating, courting, or going out, it says a great deal about relationships in general. In addition, several New Testament writers address men and women directly as well as husbands and wives. But before we jump into those specifics, let me make one observation. I'm amazed how often men attempt to leverage the passages addressing women to get the women in their lives to change or to behave differently. And yes, I've talked to my share of wives through the years who are quick to remind their husbands what the New Testament says about being a "good husband."

Why bring this up to my primarily unwed audience? It underscores something you otherwise may not believe. Namely, the right person myth extends right on into marriage. The assumption of husbands and wives who leverage the Bible to modify spousal behavior is: "If I could get my spouse to act *right*, everything would be *all right*." Odd thing, these are the very couples who married assuming they had met the *right person* to begin with. Turns out, the *right person* doesn't always act *right*. So what do they do? Look in the mirror and work on themselves? Heck no. They didn't do that when they were dating; why start now? Instead they go to work trying to *fix* their spouses. Nobody wants to be *fixed*. *Fix* your pet, not your partner.

Sounds like a bumper sticker.

People don't get married to be *fixed*. They get married to be loved. Or fed. Moral of the story: single people who refuse to focus on *becoming the person the person they're looking for is looking for* become spouses who don't focus on becoming the spouses their partners were hoping for.

Don't do that.

Abandoning the right person myth now will save you a

truckload of unnecessary grief later. Decide to *become* someone now so you won't have to *fix* someone later.

Back to the New Testament.

Make Love a Verb

The most transformational teaching in the New Testament
related to relationships revolves around the use of the term
love. When discussing love, New Testament writers talk
about it in terms of something one *does* as opposed to how
one *feels*. While most of us were content to merely *fall* in
love, New Testament authors instruct us to *behave* in love.
We're told to make love a verb. Jesus went so far as to use it
as an imperative. In the Gospels, he reiterated the famous
Old Testament imperative to *love our neighbors as ourselves*.
But he went a step further. He instructed his followers to
love their enemies (Matthew 5:44)! Clearly he wasn't talking
about love as most of us know it. He was referring to the
verb version: a decision to do something in spite of how we
feel. The verb form of love is the hallmark of the Christian
faith. It's also the hallmark of all great relationships. Great
relationships are built on good decisions, not strong emotion. Again, falling in love is easy; it requires a pulse. Staying
in love requires more. Specifically, embracing love as a verb.

As simple and perhaps as obvious as that sounds, it's
actually neither. If it were simple and obvious, everybody
would approach love this way. There would be far fewer
divorces, less domestic violence, and not nearly as many children wondering why Mommy or Daddy doesn't live with

them anymore. As commonsense as it may sound, the idea of embracing love as a verb is not all that common. Our culture is not characterized by love as a verb or an imperative. Our culture is characterized by a multifaceted distortion of the Golden Rule:

- Do unto others as they do unto you.
- Do unto others as they deserve to be done unto.
- Do unto others so as to get them to do what you want them to do.
- Do unto others until you are ready to do unto somebody else.

Such are the unwritten rules of too many relationships. The assumption being, "I'll do my part as long as you do yours." The results are fragile relational contracts built on conditional agreements that leave both parties focused on the behavior of their partner. To borrow a phrase from my friend Craig Groeschel, they are relationships built on "mutual distrust."

All this is a direct outflow of the right person myth. People expect their *right persons* to act the *right way*. So they keep their eyes on 'em to make sure they uphold their end of the bargain. In a relationship where both parties expect the behavior of the other to carry the weight of the relationship, disappointment is inevitable. With disappointment comes blame. Know how many relationship problems have been solved through blame? Well yes, you do. None. Add to this our culture's low threshold for relational pain and you understand why so many people conclude their *right persons* weren't right after all. They cut their losses, chalk it up to a bad decision, and begin looking for the next *right person*.

But there's a better way. Namely, make love a verb.

Nobody said it better than Jesus:

> "A *new* command I give you: Love one another."
>
> (JOHN 13:34, emphasis added)

"But wait," you say, "why are we talking about Jesus in a book about dating when neither Jesus nor his parents ever went on a date?" Hang on. You'll see.

The Greek term translated *new* in our English Bibles connotes *strange* or *remarkable*. What made Jesus' command strange and remarkable was his inclusion of love as part of a command. He used the imperative form of the verb. Imagine Jesus as marriage counselor. Jesus: "Quit arguing, go home, and *love* each other."

Jesus didn't command his followers to feel something. He commanded them to *do* some things. But Jesus didn't stop with making love an imperative. He took it a step further. In one statement he dismantled both his ancient and our modern tit-for-tat approach to love. He introduced the world to a concept that would serve as the foundation of what would eventually become known as *Christian marriage*. He said, "As I have loved you, so you must love one another" (John 13:34). In other words, "Do unto others as I have done unto you." That's a whole 'nother kind of love, one which introduces a new and improved dynamic to any relationship. Here's why. As long as I love you the way you love me, my love is conditional. No way around it. I'm forced into the role of monitor as well as lover. But if I choose to love you the way someone else loves me, and that person loves me well, your response to my love becomes almost inconsequential. I'm not doing unto you as you do unto me. I'm doing unto you as someone else has done unto me.

Fast Forward

A few years after Jesus took his leave, his first-century followers began contextualizing his teaching for a non-Jewish audience. The apostle Paul, in particular, took Jesus' teaching on love and applied it to several categories of relationships, including husbands and wives. His opening statement on this topic is what I alluded to earlier as the world's most powerful relational dynamic. Here's what he wrote to the Jesus-followers in Ephesus:

> Submit to one another out of reverence for Christ.
>
> (EPHESIANS 5:21)

Amazing, huh?

No?

With these nine English words Paul introduces us to what I call *the principle of mutual submission*. I realize the term *submit* doesn't play well in our culture. Understandably so. Who wants to submit? But that's unfortunate because *submission* unlocks the door to mutually beneficial and enjoyable relationships.

The term *submit* literally means "to subordinate or place oneself under the authority of another." Can't wait. What could be more enjoyable than handing control of my life over to someone else? But Paul wasn't calling for an unequivocal, unilateral abandonment of personal independence. This is a *one another* thing:

> Submit to *one another* ...
>
> (emphasis added)

In a relationship characterized by mutual submission, both parties choose to submit themselves to the other. This is a two-way avenue. Mutual submission doesn't work unless it's mutual. It only *works* when both parties work it. But like Jesus, Paul didn't stop there.

> Submit to one another out of reverence for Christ.

Paul didn't instruct the believers in Ephesus to submit to one another out of reverence for one another. Let's face it, most "one anothers" you know don't deserve your submission. Paul takes us back to the dynamic Jesus introduced. The phrase "out of reverence for Christ" suggests that we are to submit to one another out of reverence for the fact that Christ submitted himself to each of us when he leveraged his life to pay our sin debt. His sacrifice is to serve as the inspiration and standard for our submission to one another. What does that look like? Specifically, what does that look like between individuals who have committed their lives to each other in marriage? Paul knew we would wonder. Here's what he said:

> Wives, submit yourselves to your own husbands as you do to the *Lord*.
>
> (EPHESIANS 5:22, emphasis added)

> Husbands, love your wives, just as *Christ* loved the church and gave himself up for her.
>
> (EPHESIANS 5:25, emphasis added)

Depending on what you saw growin' up or what you've experienced as a grown-up, that may sound completely unrealistic. Too idealistic. But before you pass it off too quickly, here's something to consider: What's the alternative? What are your options? Remain guarded? Love only as you are loved? Give only as you are given to? Trust only to the degree you are trusted? The alternative is to invite *fear* into future relationships. Fear that will undermine intimacy. Fear that will keep you from giving yourself wholly to another person out of concern for how he or she might, or might not, respond. While your reservation is perfectly understandable, it's entirely unnecessary and counterproductive. You were created for more than guarded relationships and "I will as long as you will" love. Truth is, you hope that's true, even if you've never seen it or experienced it.

The apostle John, a man who knew Jesus as well as anyone, wrote:

> There is no fear in love. But *perfect* love drives out fear.
>
> (1 JOHN 4:18, emphasis added)

Perfect love is love expressed through mutual submission. Mutual submission is an expression of fearless love that, in turn, drives out fear. It is a decision to trust, to put the other person first regardless. I've witnessed the transformational power of this unique approach to love on many occasions. But one in particular stands out.

When I was twenty-six, I flew to Washington, D.C., to be a groomsman in a friend's wedding. After the reception, the wedding party of twelve or so headed to an upscale bar in Georgetown. Being part of the wedding party, I tagged along. Most of us had met only two days earlier when we arrived for the festivities. Everybody ordered a drink. I ordered a cheeseburger. Which of course attracted some unwanted attention. I'm not sure why. Most of 'em spent most of the reception drinking. I had spent most of the reception eating. Why switch horses in midstream?

Eventually, the attractive girl next to me asked why I didn't drink. Her exact question was, "So Andy, why don't you drink? Is it a religious thing?" Since she'd been drinking quite a lot, half the table heard her and paused for my answer. Because we were at a wedding, I decided to give my best wedding answer. "Well," I said, "I figure if I don't drink, it will give my future wife one less thing to worry about." Little did I know that she came from a home split by her father's abuse of alcohol. One question led to another and the next thing I knew we were having a friendly debate about gender roles in marriage. By "we" I mean everybody at my end of the table. By "debate" I mean it was everybody at my end of the table versus me. Fortunately, I was sober. But they were louder.

The turning point in the conversation came when the girl next to the girl who started all of this said, and I quote, "Andy, I heard a preacher say that the man had to be the head of the home because a two-headed home is like a two-headed monster. Is that what you believe? That the man is the head?"

There's a verse somewhere in the New Testament where Jesus says that if you are arrested and put on trial for what you believe, God will give you the words to say. While I hadn't been arrested, I certainly felt like I was on trial. So I shot up one of those "I need words to say" prayers, and God was gracious. Both girls passed out and had to be taken outside for fresh air.

Not really.

Here's the gist of what I said. Or, heard myself saying. And this was directed at the girls who were asking the questions.

"Before I answer your question, imagine you're married to a man who genuinely believes you are the most fantastic person on the planet. He's crazy about you. You have no doubt that your happiness is his top priority. He listens when you talk. He honors you in public. To use an old fashioned term, he 'cherishes' you. He's not afraid to make a decision. He values your opinions. He leads, but he listens. He's responsible. He's not argumentative. You have no doubt that he would give his life for you if the need arose. You never worry about him being unfaithful. In fact, to quote an old Flamingos' song, he only has eyes for you."

As I was saying all of this, the folks on the other end of the table tuned in and began to listen. I went on and on describing pretty much the perfect guy. The longer I talked, the more I sensed their resistance ebbing. When I finished, I paused and asked, "Would either of you have trouble following a man like that?" The girl to my right blurted out, "Well, hell no! I want to meet that guy." Everybody laughed.

Without realizing it, she made my point. It's easy, perhaps natural, to submit to someone who genuinely has your best interest in mind. There's no *fear*. No reason to resist. Conversely, anyone who has your best interest in mind has in effect submitted to you. That person has chosen to leverage him- or herself for your benefit, basically saying, "You first."

This is the love you were made for. And it's possible. My hope is that you would begin believing it's possible for YOU. And that once you've accepted this possibility, you would get to work *becoming* rather than simply *looking*. If you were to find someone who had prepared to love you like that, but you hadn't done the hard work of preparing to love that way in return, it wouldn't work, would it? Stand-alone submission is dangerous. But *mutual* submission? That's different. A relationship characterized by *mutual submission* is the best of all possible relationships. It is a relationship worth *preparing* for.

It is a relationship worth *waiting* for.

CHAPTER 5

LOVE IS

When we finish a novel or film centered around two people finding happiness in each other's arms, we assume they lived happily ever after whether the author or director says so or not. Translated: After a temporary season of hardship and adversity, everything was good from that point forward. Nothing else that happened was worth writing about. Don't wait for the sequel. There won't be one. Once they found the right person, everything was all right.

We know better. Real life isn't that way. Heck, your real life hasn't been that way. But there's something in all of us that continues to cling to the hope that we will be the exception, that we will meet the *right person* and live happily ever after due to nothing other than having found our soul mates.

If you're not a Bible reader, you may find this hard to believe. On the subject of love, the most prolific writer in the New Testament, Paul, actually addresses our childhood fantasy of living happily ever after. As an epilogue to one of the most famous and most oft-quoted pieces of ancient literature on the subject of love, he wrote:

> When I was a child, I talked like a child, I thought like a child, I reasoned like a child. When I became a man, I put the ways of childhood behind me.
>
> (1 CORINTHIANS 13:11)

Allow me to expound. Keep in mind, this follows a description of what true love looks like and acts like:

"When I was a child, I *talked about love* like a child talks about love. I *thought about love* like a child thinks about love. When I *fantasized about what love would be like*, I fantasized like you would expect a child to fantasize. But when I grew up, I put *those childish ideas about love* behind me."

As I said, this was how Paul concluded his most famous teaching on the subject of love. His point was actually a subtle warning: if you carry childhood notions of love into adulthood, you most certainly won't live happily ever after. As we abandon childish notions about many other things, so we must abandon our storybook assumptions about love.

Think about it. Aren't you amazed at how *immature* adults can be when it comes to love and relationships? Immature, as in *childish. Childlike.* Why is that? When it comes to their relationships with women, why do grown men revert to acting like teenaged boys? And why do grown women play along? Why do adult men treat women like toys that once broken are to be abandoned for new ones? Why do women act like store-shelf commodities? Come on. We all know that approach to romance never ends well. So why is it repeated so often? Why have *you* repeated it so often?

Simple. When it comes to love and relationships, we are inclined to hold onto our childlike ways. We fail to put "the ways of childhood" behind us. Men trade their bicycles for cars but continue to believe that when it comes to girls, charm is enough. Women trade their dolls for a closet full of fashion but continue to believe that the "mirror, mirror on the wall will result in a life of happiness after all." In the end, nobody lives happily ever after. Worse, many conclude there's no such thing as happily ever after. But they're wrong. There's another way. But embracing it requires that we let go of our childish ways, our childish approach to relationships. To quote your momma, "It's time for you to grow up!"

So, having looked at Paul's conclusion, let's rewind to the beginning of his commentary on love. In his letter to Christians living in Corinth, a city in ancient Greece, he gives us a beautiful and exhaustive explanation of how genuine love looks and behaves. These words may sound familiar. They are read in weddings every weekend in churches, backyards, ballrooms, and wherever else weddings are sold.

I mean, held.

No, I mean sold.

Paul's description of love serves as detailed commentary on the concept of mutual submission. His words line up precisely with Jesus' command to make love a verb. As we are about to discover, Paul breaks love down into a whole list of verbs. Whereas we grow up fantasizing about how the person we fall in love with will make us feel, Paul points us in a different direction. But for all you romantics out there, there's good news. When two people love like Paul suggests we love, the result is often the very thing you imagined romantic love to be when you first began imagining such things. This approach to love is your best hope for eliciting in your partner the *feeling* you hope your partner will elicit in you. There's a cause and effect in love. When both people are willing to do a little *causing*, both experience a little *effecting*. Perhaps *affection* would be a better word. When two people choose to put the other first, powerful things transpire. So, leveraging Jesus' teaching on love, Paul gives us the grown-up version of what love really is.

> Love is patient,
> love is kind.
> It does not envy,
> it does not boast,
> it is not proud.
> It does not dishonor others,
> it is not self-seeking,
> it is not easily angered,
> it keeps no record of wrongs.
> Love does not delight in evil but rejoices with the truth.
> It always protects, always trusts, always hopes, always
>   perseveres.
> Love never fails.
>
> (1 CORINTHIANS 13:4–8)

So, there's your *to become* list. Master the art of love the way Paul describes it and you are good to go. Find someone cute who has mastered it and who feels the same way about you that you do about him, and the two of you are good to go. You'll probably live happily ever after. If your initial mental response is something along the lines of, *I'm not so sure. I'll never be all of that*; if once again you're tempted to close this book and move on to whatever's next on your reading list, do us both a quick favor. Look back over the list and circle the qualities you're not looking for in a future partner. If you're currently in a relationship, circle the qualities you're willing to give your partner a pass on, the ones you would be willing to tell your partner aren't really important to you.

I'll wait.

I'm guessing you didn't remove too many items from the list. So here's what I suggest. Now that you know what you're expecting of him or her, maybe those should be the things you begin working on yourself. Now that you've narrowed the list of what you're looking for, you know what to become so that the person you're looking for will be looking for you. If you hope your current or future partner is not "self-seeking," then that would be a good thing for you to focus on. If you hope he or she "always trusts," then perhaps you should dig in and start working on your own trust issues. In other words, *become the person the person you're looking for is looking for.* Or at a minimum, don't expect more of that person than you expect of yourself.

Childish love says, "If I find someone who's as crazy about me as I am about him, everything on that list will just magically happen … as I wish upon a star." You know better. Do impatient people suddenly become patient simply because they've fallen in love? No, they may exhibit patience in order to get what they want. But that's more *predator* than *patience*. Genuine patience is not a means to an end.

Do people with trust issues find themselves overcome with a natural inclination toward trust simply because they've met the right person? No. Unresolved daddy-and-momma issues have the power to squash the trust right out of a relationship within the first nine to twelve months. Again, anybody can exhibit trust short-term in order to impress or persuade. But like patience, like everything on Paul's list, trust is not a means to a selfish end. It's the very opposite.

So, with that in mind, let's work our way through Paul's list. While it might feel a bit ideal and unattainable, we would all agree most items on his list are on *our* lists when it comes to the person we're looking for.

Patient

"Love is patient" (1 Corinthians 13:4). Patience is the *decision* to move at someone else's pace rather than pressure him or her to match yours. Patience is choosing to do less than you are capable of for the sake of keeping in step with someone else. Now, if all we were talking about was an afternoon jog or a walk on the beach, that would be easy. But *pace* refers to lots of things. The pace of conversation. The pace of understanding. The pace at which a person makes decisions. The pace of getting ready to go out. The pace of career advancement. The pace at which someone is ready to become a parent. The pace at which a person is ready to make a lifetime commitment. The pace at which an individual is ready to take a relationship to the next level. Patience is a *decision* to *pause* rather than *push*.

Impatience is different. Impatience isn't a decision, is it? It's an emotion. It's something you *feel*. Kind of like *love* is something you feel. Isn't that interesting? You can *feel* love and *feel* impatient. In fact, you can *feel* impatient with someone you love. The feeling of impatience can actually trump and interfere with those loving feelings, can't they? The reverse is also true. *Feeling* pressured by someone who claims to love you can crush your loving feelings as well. That's a big deal.

Patience isn't natural. Your *natural pace* is *natural*. Your natural instinct is to assume that your pace is *the* pace by which all paces should be judged. Right? So, you think he's impatient and he thinks you're slow. She thinks you should be moving up in the company faster and you feel pressured. Love, as expressed through patience, never pressures another person to speed up in order to satisfy a desire to move at one's natural pace. Love defers. Love defers to the pace of the other. Love creates and allows for as much space, time, and margin as the other person needs. Love never says, "If you love me, you'll step it up!" Love says, "Because I love you, I'll gear down. I'll move at your pace." Like everything in Paul's list, patience is simply a way of putting the other person first. Patience is an expression of submission. Your pace, not mine.

Do you struggle with im-patience? Do you expect the people around you to move at your pace? To work at your pace? To catch on to things as quickly as you do? Do you feel like you're constantly revving your internal engines while waiting for everybody else to "get with it"? Then you have some work to do. But think of it as an investment. Learning to gear down now will prepare you to gear down later. And rest assured, no matter how competent and talented your future partner is, you'll need to have a well-exercised patience muscle. So start now. Decide to move at the pace of the people around you. That's what love *does*.

Kind

Next up, *kindness*. Paul writes, "Love is patient. Love is kind" (1 Corinthians 13:4). Kindness feels soft. Weak. But not so. To be kind is to *leverage one's strength on behalf of another*. When we're kind, we put our strength, abilities, and resources on loan to someone who lacks them. When you're kind, you put *you* at someone's disposal. Kindness is powerful. Kindness, like patience, is a decision. It's the decision to do for others what they cannot in that moment do for themselves. Kindness, in its purest form, is unconditional. It's not a means to a personal end. The goal of kindness is to benefit the person to whom it's extended. *Kindness is love's response to weakness*. Kindness is perhaps the most important component in a romantic relationship.

How's that?

Unkindness kills romance. Instantly. I don't care how deeply you feel for someone, a small dose of unkindness will douse the flames of romance in a nanosecond. Consistent doses of unkindness eventually destroy a relationship. Perhaps you've seen or even experienced that. Everybody knows how to be kind when kindness has a potential reward attached Right? Everybody's kind on the first date. Every-body's kind when there's something to be gained. The question you need to answer is: What is your natural response to weakness in the people closest to you? Do you lean in? Or do you power up? Do you loan your strength? Or do you expect people to match your strength?

Ladies and gentlemen, pay close attention to how a potential future partner responds to those he or she perceives as weak. Eventually he or she will perceive a weakness in you. You will expect that potential partner to lean in and loan you some strength. But that will only happen if said person has developed the habit of opting for kindness in the face of weakness. And while I'm delving into your personal life, *unkindness* doesn't dissipate with the introduction of sex or a ring. In fact, odds are good, it will escalate. People who use kindness as a means to an end are often mean in the end.

Moving right along.

Love Does Not

"Love is patient, love is kind." Paul continues, "It does not envy, it does not boast, it is not proud" (1 Corinthians 13:4). Quite the threesome. He groups these together because they're related, as expressions of insecurity. When they surface in a relationship, they are ugly, petty, and destructive. Envy, boasting, and pride undermine the foundations of a relationship. Like unkindness, they kill romance. This toxic trio is expressed in relationships by way of sarcasm, criticism, and public disrespect. The idea of *envy* in a dating or otherwise romantic relationship may seem foreign. But remember, *success can be threatening*. A man or woman's individual success will eventually find its way into the fissures of his or her partner's insecurity. Like frozen water in the invisible cracks of a sidewalk, what was once invisible eventually becomes visible — to all. No doubt you've met successful people whose spouses can't find a positive word to say about them. You wonder, *Where is that coming from?* Instead of celebrating each other's strengths and successes, they tear at each other.

Here's something you need to know, something you dare not lose sight of as you evaluate a current or future relationship. The roots of envy always run deeper and wider than the relationship in which it surfaces. In other words, if your partner is envious of you, if he always has to one-up you, if she struggles to say anything good about you publicly, it's not your fault. And ... if you find it hard to compliment your partner in public, if you have a tendency to find fault, it ain't your partner's fault. Again, the roots of envy always run deeper and wider than the relationships in which they surface. While envy may have surfaced in your relationship, it certainly wasn't caused by it. This makes envy next to impossible to deal with. After all, it's not a relationship problem. It's one of those individual problems smuggled into the relationship. If I don't feel good about me, I can't let you feel too good about you. Since I can't pull me up, I'll find ways to drag you down. That's the way envy works. That's why it's relationally toxic.

So, here's some advice: pay attention to your internal reaction to the success of the people closest to you. Is your initial response to *celebrate* or *denigrate*? To add to or subtract from? Are you comfortable allowing the spotlight to remain on other people? Or do you find yourself scrambling for a way to direct the attention in your direction? Envy is next to impossible to see in the mirror. But if you pay attention, you may see it mirrored in your relationships. If you do, rest assured, it's your issue. *To become the person the person you are looking for is looking for,* you've got to own it and dethrone it.

So what do you do when it dawns on you that you have envy issues? Simple. You ignore your initial impulse to criticize or grab the spotlight and instead you *celebrate*. You don't stay neutral. You don't bite your tongue. You initiate. You engage. Public celebration is the best way to bridle the envy and jealousy that reside in your heart, the envy that you *bring* to the relationship that you otherwise might be tempted to think was *caused* by the relationship. Instead of attempting to tell a better story, you listen and say: "Really? A three-pound bass—you caught a three-pound bass. That's great!" You don't interrupt to remind everybody that your dad has a show on the Fishing Channel. You don't tell *your* story. You celebrate his.

Face it. If you don't feel good about yourself, criticizing somebody else isn't going to fix that, is it? Sarcasm isn't a strategy for self-improvement. Tearing someone down doesn't actually build you up. So stop with all that. The person you're looking for isn't looking for that any more than you are. Yes, you may have some work to do in this area, but that's okay. You're still becoming. And—and this is a big *and*—the thing that will keep you from doing what I suggest is one of the toxic trio: pride. Pride is what keeps us from celebrating what others have accomplished. Pride is what causes us to keep our mouths shut when we should be pouring on the praise.

Now, I know what some of you are thinking at this point: "Andy, this is starting to sound like the worst date ever. We'll start out the night by being really patient with each other. Then we'll take turns being kind. Next we'll drive around and not envy each other. At the end of the evening, neither of us will boast. And then the next morning we can pride ourselves in not being proud. Sounds awesome. Great book." I deserve that. But keep reading. Not because it gets any better. I just think you ought to finish what you start.

Dis-Honoring

So far we've discovered love is patient, kind, and it doesn't envy or boast. Next on Paul's list: love "does not dishonor" (1 Corinthians 13:5). *Honor* is a term we don't use much. Worse, honor is a dynamic we don't see illustrated often in relationships. But honor is at the heart of every great relationship. In fact, if you fall in love with someone who has prepared to, and is committed to, honoring you, you are one lucky individual. In some ways, honor is the epicenter of a satisfying relationship. Like the other descriptors on Paul's list, honor is something you choose to do. It's a decision. To understand honor we need to step outside the realm of romance for a couple of paragraphs.

Imagine winning an expensive dinner at the finest restaurant in town with your favorite actor, actress, recording artist, or author. If you don't have a favorite, choose from among your favorites. Think for a moment about the preparation you would make and the way you would behave. That's honor. You would bring your best version of you to the occasion. You would think through what you were going to wear. You would show up early. If your hero arrived late, you wouldn't mention it. You would pay careful attention to what you said and how you said it. You would insist he or she sit in a choice seat and order first. You may call someone on the way for a quick review of table etiquette. You know, dinner fork versus dessert fork. You would laugh at the person's jokes, ask questions, and do your best to be engaging. You would be appropriately self-conscious. In every way imaginable, you would put your hero's interests ahead of your own. Why? Because this is someone you respect. And your respect for what he or she has accomplished would push you to be the best version of you possible. Making your best effort to be the best possible version of you is an expression of honor.

Here's another one.

This time I want you to think about your most prized possession. Your car? A piece of jewelry? Something you built? A signed photo of the person you just imagined sharing dinner with? That thing you would try to save first in a fire. Got it? Now think about the way you handle or treat that particular item. Think about how you would feel, or have felt, if someone mishandled it or treated it way too casually. The word that captures those emotions is *protective*. We protect and safeguard the things we ascribe value to. That also is an expression of honor. At the end of Paul's description of love, he uses that very term. He says, "Love always protects." Protecting is an expression of honor. I had an expensive guitar once that I would only allow other people to play while I was in the room. I took it out of the case and I put it back. Then I locked it and hid the key. You probably had similar feelings about your first car. Especially if it was a new car. We are protective of the things we honor.

So honor is about bringing the best version of you to a relationship. Honor involves expressing value through protection. But there is a third facet to honor that deserves attention. Honor *defers*. Honor *yields*. Honor gives way.

Honor takes every opportunity to express, "You first." Interesting thing, Paul doesn't present *honor* as something to aspire to. He presents it as something we should never deviate from. Paul says, "Love does not dishonor." Love never steps down. Honor isn't love on a particularly good day. Honor is every day.

If you've spent time with a couple that honors each other, you know how powerful this single facet of love can be. Admittedly, it's rare. It's rare because there's a voice in our heads that whispers, "But isn't honor earned? Shouldn't I reserve honor for honorable people?" The answer to both questions is no. Honor is a decision. It's a choice. Honor is what love does. Have you ever had someone you cared about behave dishonorably toward you? It was his choice, wasn't it? You can choose to honor, as the person you love can choose to honor you. Mutual honor creates a culture of respect that makes it easy to believe the best. Love, verb-love, chooses to show honor. It doesn't dishonor.

It breaks my heart to see men or women remain in relationships where they are repeatedly dishonored. It breaks my heart because I know, over time, a dishonored person will conclude that she is in fact dishonorable. Dishonor can begin to feel normal. Comfortable. As a Christian, I believe you were made in the image of God. That makes you inherently honorable. Your honor rests not on your behavior but on that divine spark that resides inside you. My hope is that you wouldn't spend one unnecessary minute allowing anyone to treat you dishonorably. And I hope you never waste a minute of your life dishonoring anyone else.

Self-Seeking

So the verb version of love is patient, kind, humble, and honoring. Next on this list, love is "not self-seeking." If this sounds like another way of saying what Paul has already said, it's because it is. The King James Version of this text reads, love "seeketh not her own." A fancy way of saying, love puts the interests and needs of other people first. If that scares you, it should. Deciding to be "not self-seeking" is risky. But honestly, early in a relationship, being self-seeking is even more dangerous. Here's why. Determining not to be self-seeking is the quickest way to determine just how self-seeking your love interest is. Yes, you read that right. Resisting this application of love prolongs the discovery process. If you give and give and give and the other person takes and takes and takes, then you'll know to run and run and run. But if you choose not to be self-seeking and your love interest returns the favor, then you've made a valuable discovery.

Provocative

The next descriptor Paul gives us is a bit odd. Some modern translations read "not easily angered." As you probably know, the New Testament was originally written in Greek. The Greek term Paul chose is probably best translated *provoked* or *stirred*. This term was used in the context of cooking. We have a similar idea in the English language. We say things like, "By the time he finished lecturing me, I was so stirred up that I wanted to punch him." We have other figures of speech that reflect Paul's meaning:

- "She knows how to push my buttons."
- "He knows how to set me off."
- "She got me so wound up, I had to leave until I calmed down."

Assuming you don't need any further clarification of what Paul is talking about, let's move on to the point he's making: Love doesn't get stirred up, wound up, set off, or ticked off. Love doesn't have a short fuse. Love can sit and listen and absorb and keep things in perspective. Love doesn't react. Love responds. To which you may be tempted to respond, "That's easy for you to say because you don't know (name of person who stirs you up)." That's true. Here's something equally true. Stir-ees always blame the stir-ers.

Always. But blame is lame. No one has ever blamed her way into a preferred future. Blame ensures you will live your life at the mercy of anyone with a stir stick. It will never be your fault and you'll never get any better. A winning combination. Come on, we've only known each other for five chapters, but I know you don't want to live like that. Do you? Face it, he may push your buttons, but those are *your* buttons. She may tick you off, but those are *your* ticks. Ticks? Not sure that translates as well.

Anyway.

When someone's words stir something inside of you, remember, it's inside *you*. That makes it a *you* issue. You need to own it. Love owns it and goes to work on it. Besides, what are your options? You can't run away from every relationship that has the potential to stir you up. You don't want to spend your life blaming the stir-ers. Your best option is to own it and deal with it. After all, isn't that what you want the person you're looking for to do when he gets stirred up? You're not looking for a runner. You're certainly not looking for a blamer. You're looking for someone who is *not easily angered*. Someone who is *not provoked*.

Consider this. What happens when two people who stir up bad things in each other own their individual issues rather than point fingers? Good things happen. Great things. But once the blame games begin ... well, you've seen what happens. Nothing gets resolved. The argument may eventually end, but nobody wins. Everybody walks away justified and isolated. Vindicated, but alone. You don't want that. So, start paying close attention to the things that tee and tick you off. Take note of the stir sticks that tweak your emotions quicker than they should. Once you see patterns, go to work. That's how you *become the person the person you're looking for is looking for.*

Three more to go.

Need a break?

No?

Okay, let's keep moving.

Record Keepers

Paul insists that love "keeps no record of wrongs." Another translation reads: Love "does not take into account a wrong suffered" (NASB). Were either of your parents record keepers? You know, every time they argued, the record keeper would open his or her mental file cabinet and start reading old transcripts, recounting in detail the sins of the past. Not his or her own, of course. That's the funny thing about relational record keepers. They rarely keep track of their own mistakes and indiscretions. No time for that. They're too busy filing away the misdeeds of the people around them. You're left with the impression they actually enjoy pulling out that stuff and rehashing it. They enjoyed catching the other spouse messing up. It's like they expected it. Looked for it. Then filed it away for later.

Odds are they kept a record of *your* less-than-perfect behavior as well.

This was the parent who was never content to simply discipline you for a current infraction but always attached the present to the past, leaving you to feel that you could never do anything right. He or she just couldn't stop the urge to connect all the dots as far back as either of you could remember.

"Honey, you've always had a problem with ..."

"Sweetheart, last year at this time we had the same conversation ..."

"Why do you always ...?"

"Why can't you ever ...?"

Fun times.

If you grew up with a record keeper, you're painfully aware of the negative relational dynamic that record keeping creates. What you may not be aware of is that you are prone to follow suit. You may have hated it, but you may be predisposed to repeat it. If you grew up with one, you may have to fight not to become one. Perhaps you've already become one. Funny how that happens. We know we're going to look like one of our parents. It never dawns on us that we will probably act like one of them as well. In fact, in some instances, we swear we won't. But we do. Unless we *decide* not to.

The challenge for record keepers is that they are right. Their husbands or wives, their sons and daughters, actually did all those things they remember in such vivid detail. The problem isn't their accuracy. The problem is the damage it does to a relationship. Rehearsing the past does nothing to alter or improve the future. Besides, we all know what we did in the past. We don't need to be reminded.

Do behavioral dots need to be connected? Do patterns

need to be examined? Sure. By request only. By a counselor. By a friend over coffee. But not by a spouse or significant other. Filing doesn't foster love. Forgiving and pretending to forget are your best bets for sustained romance. I say pretending because, well because, there are some things we won't ever forget. But there's no point in bringing them up. Think about it in the context of everything else we've said about love thus far. Love is not about powering up. Love is about stepping down. Love is about elevating someone else. When someone holds your past over you, who's in the elevated position? Who has the power? Who's in control? That's right, the person with the filing cabinet. Rehearsing someone's past is a power play. When you open the filing cabinet, you elevate yourself.

Love chooses not to keep dousing the present with the past. Besides, it doesn't do any good. It doesn't move the relationship forward. If one of your parents was a record keeper, I suspect you gravitated relationally toward your other parent, didn't you? Whose influence were you most open to? The filer's or the forgiver's? Who did you *feel* closest to? The filer or the forgetter? Funny how that works. Nobody gravitates toward humiliation. The path to influence is paved by acceptance, not truth.

A person can be exactly right and end up exactly alone. Filers can always justify their *truth telling*, but eventually they will *truth* the life right out of their most valued relationships. You don't want to be reminded of your failures. Your love interest doesn't want to be reminded either. So stop with all that.

On a lighter note, Sandra's mom has the opposite problem. She'll discover something Sandra's dad has done and get mad, but by the time he gets home in the afternoon she's forgotten what she was mad about. Drives her crazy. Recently she decided she should create some reminders. Seriously. Please don't tell her I told you this. Not too long ago, Bob sent a landscaper over to trim their hedges. He likes 'em trimmed to a nub so he only has to pay once per season. Jackie hates it when he does that because, well, you can imagine why. For the next two months it looks like locusts descended on their front yard. So when she heard power trimmers buzzing like hornets, she ran out and chased everybody off. Unfortunately, they had already done a good bit of damage. Or the way Bob saw it, they had only done half the work he was paying them for. Anyway, she was mad. So she called Sandra to complain. The conversation went something like this:

JACKIE: "I'm so mad. He does this every year and he knows I don't like the way it looks."

SANDRA: "Well, Mom, you need to tell him."

JACKIE: "I did. Last year. But when he gets home I'm going to tell him again."

SANDRA: "Good."

JACKIE: "Problem is, I always forget to be mad. So I locked the back door. That way, when I hear him fumbling with the lock, it'll remind me to be mad."

SANDRA: "Really? Mom, if you can't remember to be mad, I don't think you are really all that mad."

JACKIE: (chuckle) "You're right. Hold on. I'm going to unlock the door."

I've known Jackie and Bob for twenty-seven years. They have the *keeps no score of wrongs done* down to a science. In fact, they pretty much have everything in this chapter down. They've been married for fifty-plus years. They are so in love. Their kids, grandkids, as well as their two sons and daughter-in-law, love to be with them. We've had twenty-seven-plus drama-free vacations with the entire crew. If you asked them what their secret is, Bob will smile and say, "Yes dear. Yes dear." Jackie will tell you straight up, "I can't remember to be mad."

Believing Is Seeing

Paul's final descriptors are best taken together as one big, game-changing idea. In some ways, he saved the best for last when he wrote:

> Love does not delight in evil but rejoices with the truth. It always protects, always trusts, always hopes, always perseveres.
>
> (1 CORINTHIANS 13:6–7)

My summary of Paul's thoughts: Love chooses to *see* the best and *believe* the best while choosing to *overlook* the rest. It rhymes if you say it right. The phrase "does not delight in evil" takes us back to the previous section. Love does not delight in or get its kicks digging up dirt or catching someone doing wrong. Love isn't looking for or expecting bad behavior. Love is hopeful. Paul contrasts "delight in evil" with "rejoices with truth." Most English translations choose the word *truth* here. The problem is, this is a contrast. The opposite of *evil* isn't *truth*. The Greek term translated *truth* can also be translated *uprightness*, which is in fact the flip side of evil. His point? Love *looks for and celebrates good behavior*. Unlike the record keepers, love loves to catch people doing the right thing. Love goes so far as to look for excuses to credit others with right behavior. Everything that follows underscores how far love is willing to bend in order to see and believe the best:

> ... it *always* protects, *always* trusts, *always* hopes, *always* perseveres.

> (emphasis added)

Extreme, huh? Always trusts? Always? Yep. Always. A more literal translation says, "bears all things, believes all things, hopes all things, endures all things." Again, extreme. "All things." Borders on denial. You've heard the phrase, "Love is blind." Paul would agree. Actually, Paul suggests true love *chooses* to be blind. Love *chooses* not to focus on failure. Love *chooses* to celebrate success.

In every relationship there are occasional (or not so occasional) gaps or lapses. Gaps between promises and performance. Gaps between expected behavior and actual behavior.

- "She said she would be home at seven o'clock, but she pulled in at eight."

- "He said he would only be out two nights this week, but he was gone for three."
- "He said he would call as soon as he got to the hotel, and it's 1:00 a.m."

You get the picture. You have your own pictures.

Every gap gets filled with something. Every time your spouse, boyfriend, girlfriend, or friend-friend makes a promise or sets an expectation and doesn't come through, he or she creates a gap. Whether you realize it or not, you choose what goes in the gap. And there are only two choices: trust or suspicion. You either believe the best or suspect the worst. It's a choice. Paul's point is that love chooses to believe the best and hope the best. He says love "always protects." That is, when there's a gap, love does everything possible to protect the integrity of the relationship rather than undermine it with suspicion. He says love "perseveres." The term *persevere* implies stress or tension. Love continues to love when there's reason not to. Love continues to hope and trust when circumstances argue otherwise. Love opts for the most generous explanation for the other person's behavior.

- "He's late, but I'm sure he has a good explanation."
- "She hasn't called, but I'm sure there's a good reason."
- "He forgot, but he's got so much going on and I'm so grateful for all he does."
- "She's not good with details. She'll be devastated when she realizes she stood me up."

When two people choose to consistently fill the inevitable performance gaps with trust, it creates a reinforcing current that drives the relationship in a healthy direction. Trust builds trust. Knowing that Sandra believes the best about me motivates me to be my best for her. As she fills the gaps I create with trust, I find myself working hard to be worthy of that trust. Mutual trust is a self-fulfilling prophecy. Mutual suspicion is as well. As I tell engaged couples all the time, you might as well believe the best about each other because there's nothing gained by doing otherwise.

Un-Natural

So there it is: love's to-do and to-don't list.

> Love is patient, love is kind. It does not envy, it does not boast, it is not proud. It does not dishonor others, it is not self-seeking, it is not easily angered, it keeps no record of wrongs. Love does not delight in evil but rejoices with the truth. It always protects, always trusts, always hopes, always perseveres. Love never fails.
>
> (1 CORINTHIANS 13:4–8)

Love is un-natural. Do any of these traits come naturally? Granted, we know how to turn them all on when we're winning and wooing. But love does not sustain itself *naturally*. What come naturally are passion, lust, chemistry, and that "can't wait to get you alone" feeling. But over time, all of that is eventually squashed by our unbridled, selfish, self-preserving natures.

The brand of love Paul describes is a nonnegotiable for those desiring to sustain the chemistry and romance that make the early days of a relationship so exhilarating. Romance is sustained by patience, kindness, humility, and a short memory. While none of those things come naturally, every one of them is necessary. Otherwise our wounds, insecurities, and parental implants will become the driving forces and send the relationship in a bad direction. When that happens, good-bye, chemistry. Good-bye, romance. Hello, *I guess I just haven't met the right person*. It's that kind of thinking that creates the *myth*. It's a myth to think that once you meet the *right* person, you will become a *different* person. The love of your life should bring out the best in you. But only you can prevent forest fires. Sorry. Only *you* can prevent *your* impatience, unkindness, pride, anger, and record keeping from undermining your relationship.

We began this chapter with Paul's conclusion to his description of love. As we conclude, it bears repeating:

> When I was a child, I talked like a child, I thought like a child, I reasoned like a child. When I became a man, I put the ways of childhood behind me.
>
> (1 CORINTHIANS 13:11)

Are you ready to put your adolescent view of love behind you? Are you ready to stop thinking and reasoning like an adolescent? Are you willing to abandon the assumption that once you meet the right person you will magically become a different person? Are you ready to accept responsibility for who you are and why you respond the way you do? Are you ready to do the difficult but worthwhile work of *becoming the person the person you're looking for is looking for*? I hope so. Chances are, somebody out there somewhere hopes so as well.

CHAPTER 6

GENTLEMAN'S CLUB

Dispelling the right person myth is a crucial component of altering the way you approach relationships. But the right person myth is not the *only* relational myth. In this chapter I address my male readers. Ladies, you can head on over to chapter seven if you like. However, if you choose to navigate these next few pages you'll be tempted to make this chapter required reading for the man in your life. I hope so anyway.

The point of this chapter is not to "pick on the guys." My intent is to inspire all you *guys*. Specifically, I want to inspire you to step away from simply being a *guy*. I would love for you to join the ranks of men. Men as in *gentlemen*. And not *gentlemen* as in the flashing neon sign outside a strip club. Real gentlemen don't spend their discretionary time and money in strip clubs. Don't believe me? Ask strippers. They know.

Leveraging the previous chapter, I want to inspire you to

put away your childish, adolescent ways of thinking about women. Just so you know, the woman you're looking for wants you to put away your childish, adolescent ways of thinking about women as well. For the next few paragraphs I'm going to challenge you to step away from our culture's definition of masculinity and embrace the lifestyle and attitude of a true gentleman. Don't tell the women I told you this. If you get this right, you'll be in high demand. Become a gentleman and you will be the man *most* women are looking for.

Just saying.

Our secret.

I do need to warn you about one thing. A few sentences from now you'll be tempted to write me off as old-fashioned. So let me make a preemptive strike. I may be old-fashioned, but you predate old-fashioned by centuries. You're ancient. You are so ancient you make my old-fashioned look space-age.

Here's why.

Commodities

In ancient times women were treated like commodities. In our vernacular the term *commodity* is used in economic or business contexts to describe an item with commercial value. Things such as real estate, oil, gas, gold, and silver. We place a value on these items and then use them however we want. There's no personal or emotional attachment to a commodity. A commodity is an impersonal means to a personal end.

In ancient times women were bought, sold, traded, used,

discarded, collected, promised in marriage to sons of friends, and in some cases to friends of fathers. Women had no choice. No rights. Prostitution was legal, encouraged, and in many places, part of religious tradition. In ancient Rome men used prostitutes as a form of birth control. Children were expensive and unpredictable. Multiple children meant the family fortune would be carved up into smaller pieces. Once a man had an heir, it was easier and more convenient to withhold sex from his wife and take his pleasure elsewhere. In Rome this eventually led many aristocrats to give up on marriage altogether. Things got so bad that, on at least two occasions, bills were brought before the Roman senate that would obligate Roman men to marry.

Here's where you come in.

The ancient male mind-set toward women was as much or more the result of the way men are wired as it was the times in which they lived. In other words, ancient men didn't treat women like commodities because they were ancient. They treated women like commodities because they were men. Left to our own vices, with no social or legal guardrails, that's how it would be today. How do I know? Because as *you* know, that's how it *is* today in some parts of the world. Society has evolved. Women's rights have evolved. Men have not. This is why the porn industry is recession proof. In the US it's illegal for men to own, trade, abuse, and discard women. So men can only fantasize about it. And we do. To the tune of about ten billion dollars a year.[4]

Of course, a segment of the male population in our country is not content to imagine. As we've all been reminded in recent years, there is a thriving sex trade industry in the US. The term *slave* is offensive to our modern sensibilities. But there are thousands of young women and, yes, children, who live in an invisible world that is impossible to imagine unless you've been there. In fact, the number of children sexually exploited in the US or at risk of being exploited is between 100,000 and 300,000.[5] The sex trade exists for one reason. It's profitable. And no surprise here, it's funded almost exclusively by men. Well, not really. It's funded primarily by males, not men. While we've upgraded our mode of transportation since ancient times, our approach to quenching our unquenchable lust is as sordid as it's ever been. While much about us and around us has evolved, male desire for the sexual conquest of women has remained in its primordial state. It hasn't budged. Chances are, it never will. When left to our private, unaccountable, godless selves, women are still commodities.

But let's be honest. This seedy side of maleness is not isolated to computers and clubs. It's everywhere. It's in our music and movies. It's part of every popular television series. The adage "sex sells" is a politically correct, socially acceptable way of saying, "presenting women as commodities sells." Sex doesn't sell anything. It's the promise of sex that sells. But it's not just the promise of sex. Let's be grown-ups about this. It's the promise that *this product will increase a man's potential for gratifying himself sexually with a sexually attractive woman, with the option of discarding her for another when he so chooses.* The shorter version being, *this product will empower males to behave like cavemen.*

Multiple times a day we are encouraged to think about women as commodities: take them, use them, do whatever we want with them, and then trade them for something of equal or greater value. Worse, from my perspective, is that women are usually the messengers: "Take me, use me, do anything you want with me, and then discard me or trade me in for another one." And I understand why women do this. They get paid. It's profitable. It's capitalism. Free enterprise. And just so you know, I'm not going to ask you to sign a petition or boycott anything.

So we have a bit of a problem.

Males still think like cavemen. Women are complicit. This complicit behavior ultimately undermines a man's ability to have a successful relationship with a woman. Women find that disheartening and at times disgusting.

Ancient Passion Meets Old-Fashioned

Here's something I'll bet you didn't know: Christianity introduced an entirely new paradigm for how women were to be viewed and treated. Contrary to what you may have been taught or heard, Jesus elevated the role and status of women. Significantly. When applied correctly, Christianity does as well. The apostle Paul and others introduced Jesus' revolutionary way of thinking about women to the Greco-Roman world through missionary endeavors. This new teaching was radical. Threatening. But women found it extraordinarily refreshing. Liberating. Jesus introduced several new ideas related to women. Most importantly, he taught that God loved women as much as God loved men. That's not revolutionary to us because we've heard it all our lives. But the equality of God's love for the sexes is a fundamentally Christian way of thinking. Again, don't believe me? Just do a quick mental review of what you know about how other religions allow, and in some cases encourage, men to treat women. We are deceived into thinking that we're simply more sophisticated. Wrong. We've covered that. We are not more sophisticated. Otherwise, prostitution and porn would have been sophisticatedly eradicated from our culture by now. No. We're not more sophisticated; we are more *Christian*. The value Westerners place on the individual worth and rights of women is a leftover from our Christian heritage. If you aren't a Christian, that's a bit hard to swallow. No worries. The remainder of this chapter isn't predicated on that notion. But it's certainly something to consider. Especially in light of the rights and privileges women enjoy in countries that have been influenced by Christianity or were at one time considered Christian. In fact, I'll make a prediction. As our culture, or any culture, drifts further away from a value system rooted in a Christian worldview, women and children will suffer most.

This is already the case.

Love — Even Women

In addition to teaching that God loved women as much as God loved men, Jesus taught that one's love for God was to be gauged by how well one treated other people. Again, this was new territory. On one occasion he went so far as to say that if someone was in line at the temple to make a sacrifice and remembered a relational loose end regarding a friend, family member, or business associate, he was to get out of line, go to that person, and make things right before making the sacrifice (Matthew 5:23–24). His point? A person can't be right with God and be out of sorts with people. Even female people. Unlike other religious traditions, Jesus taught that the two are not mutually exclusive. While this was unsettling within the Jewish community, it was without parallel in pagan communities. The Greek and Roman gods didn't love their worshipers. Consequently, there was no accountability to the gods for how worshipers treated their fellow man, even less for how they treated their fellow women. For Jesus to equate love for people with love for God was radical. And chicks dug it.

But it wasn't just what Jesus taught that challenged the status quo. His behavior was equally unsettling. When we read the narratives that depict Jesus' interactions with women, we filter them through our twenty-first century, American, everybody-is-born-with-certain-unalienable-rights way of thinking. Consequently, we miss the disruptive nature of these exchanges. If you grew up going to church, you're probably familiar with a narrative from John's gospel sometimes referred to as the story of the woman at the well. I won't review the entire account here. What's important for our discussion is Jesus' followers' response to catching him chatting with a woman in public. Jesus was waiting outside the Samaritan town of Sychar while his posse had gone into town to buy groceries. When they returned, they discovered him talking with a woman they'd never seen before—apparently someone from town. John, who was present at the time, recorded the following:

> Just then his disciples returned and were *surprised* to find him talking with a woman. But no one asked, "What do you want?" or "Why are you talking with her?"
>
> (JOHN 4:27, emphasis added)

The Greek term translated *surprised* is translated in other sections of John as *amazed*. One translation says they *marveled*. Men didn't talk to women alone in public. Rabbinic law taught that a man who spoke to a woman alone in public brought evil upon himself.[6] Besides, Jews didn't mix with Samaritans at all unless they absolutely had to. So for Jesus to be talking alone with a Samaritan woman was ... scandalous. But at the same time, his decision to address this woman elevated her dignity in ways we cannot fathom. More so in light of the fact that this was not just any Samaritan woman. She had a past. A past that may have explained why she chose to make her trek to the well alone instead of in the company of the other women from her village. No doubt she hesitated even to make eye contact with this Jewish man who had apparently wandered off course on his way to somewhere else.

Best we can tell, this was early in Jesus' ministry. Eventually the apostles grew accustomed to such unusual, unbecoming behavior from their Rabbi. Jesus went out of his way to elevate the status of women simply by stopping and acknowledging their presence and thus their value. When the gospel writers penned their individual accounts of Jesus' life, they ran the risk of undermining his credibility and theirs by including his interactions with women. Apparently, there were so many similar exchanges that the writers knew they could not overlook all of them and stay true to the story line. For example, if it had been possible for the gospel writers to have navigated around the fact that women first discovered and announced the resurrection, I'm sure they would have. But there was no way past the truth that it was Jesus' female followers who were up before dawn to visit the tomb. When the women ran to report his body missing, Luke tells us the men in the room responded just like you would expect men to respond:

> But they did not believe the women, because their words seemed to them like nonsense.
>
> (LUKE 24:11)

As it turned out, the women were right. This fact alone is of far more significance than our Western minds can fathom. Women were chosen as the bearers of accurate, reliable information. This, at a time in history when women were not allowed to testify in court because their testimony was considered suspect and unreliable.

Trending

What began with Jesus continued in the early church. Women were afforded unprecedented influence, freedom, and protection.[7] This was due in large part to Christian doctrine. In a letter addressed to Jesus-followers living in a city located in modern-day Turkey, Paul insists that anyone who placed his or her faith in Jesus was a child of God (Galatians 3:26). Then he makes a statement that I'm sure his first-century readers had to read more than once to ensure they had not misunderstood.

> There is neither Jew nor Greek, there is neither slave nor free man, there is neither male nor female; for you are all one in Christ Jesus.
> (GALATIANS 3:28 NASB)

To say they were all "one" was to say they were all equal. This was difficult for Jews, who assumed they were superior to Greeks. It was more difficult for citizens and freemen who viewed themselves as superior to slaves. But it was most difficult for the men. They had been taught since childhood that women were, by nature, inferior creatures. Now a man, Paul, was insisting God saw no distinction in status or value between men and women. This was radical.

But it wasn't just doctrine that elevated the status of women. The application of Jesus' teaching in the early church was extraordinarily honoring to women as well. One application in particular.

In Roman and Greek cultures, as in all ancient cultures, women were expected to be chaste before marriage and faithful to their husbands during marriage. Men had always played by a different set of rules. In the church, however, men were expected to remain sexually pure before marriage and faithful to their wives *till death they did part*. In just about every letter the apostle Paul wrote to Greek and Roman Christians, he commanded both women and men to abstain from adultery and immorality. "Flee from sexual immorality," he wrote to the believers in Corinth (1 Corinthians 6:18). It could be argued that all his exhortations to sexual fidelity were directed at Christian men. Such behavior was already expected of women. As is almost always the case.

Loophole Logic

Jesus' and Paul's teaching on divorce and remarriage was another arena in which women were given broader rights and greater respect. In the ancient world women had no means for divorcing their husbands. But men could divorce their wives for just about any reason. Jesus' most in-depth teaching on the subject of marriage was in response to a question that demonstrated how liberal the prevailing view was regarding a man's access to divorce.

> Some Pharisees came to him to test him. They asked, "Is it lawful for a man to divorce his wife for any and every reason?"
>
> (MATTHEW 19:3)

Notice the question was not, "What are acceptable grounds for divorce?" The question assumed that only men could initiate a divorce. The only question remaining was, "On what grounds?"

Jesus' response was so extreme that even today, very few

churches hold to his standard. He closed all the loopholes, raised the bar, and put men and women on equal footing in marriage. When he finished his discourse, his disciples responded in a fashion that underscores how extreme they considered his view to be. Keep in mind, these men heard every word and had a much better understanding of what he was getting at than modern scholars and theologians. Here's how Matthew remembered it:

> The disciples said to him, "If this is the situation between a husband and wife, it is better not to marry."
>
> (MATTHEW 19:10)

Jesus didn't give anybody, including the men, an out. According to Jesus, through marriage, a man and woman become one flesh. His point was unmistakably clear. Don't try to un-one what God makes one. Marriage is permanent. Thus the disciples' response. In saying this, Jesus did away with the notion that a man could walk away from his wife whenever it suited him.

And women loved it.

Handle with Care

New Testament writers didn't stop with closing marital exit ramps. They spoke to the issue of how women were to be treated within marriage. Paul instructed husbands to love their wives more than they loved their own bodies (Ephesians 5:28). Peter instructed husbands to treat their wives as "partners" and joint "heirs" or owners in God's coming kingdom. He wrote:

> Husbands, in the same way be considerate as you live
> with your wives, and treat them with respect ...
>
> (1 PETER 3:7)

First-century culture gave little consideration to women. Peter instructed Christian men to reverse that trend. To *be considerate* is to take someone into consideration. That is, factor in all you know about someone as you determine your response. Another way to translate "treat them with respect" is *grant them honor* or *treat them honorably.* Why did Peter instruct husbands to treat their wives with respect? Doesn't everybody know that? Apparently not. Again, his context was a male-dominated culture where women were commodities. So he needed to say it. But he wasn't finished.

> Husbands, in the same way be considerate as you
> live with your wives, and treat them with respect as the
> *weaker* partner ..."
>
> (emphasis added)

Weaker? Ladies, don't be offended. Peter was referring to the fact that your husband can probably beat you in an arm wrestling contest. Probably. Peter was addressing a culture of violence. A world where physical strength meant everything. His words served as a reminder to men that, while a woman lacked the physical power and value culture associated with physical strength, she was to be treated as a vessel of great value. The term translated *partner* actually means *vessel.* Whereas a man's physical strength is immediately evident, a woman's value is often hidden; it is contained within.

In a world where women were considered a means to an

end, the message of Jesus and his followers was revolutionary. It represented a cultural shift that was both uncomfortable and unsettling. In the Greco-Roman world where the gods had no love for mankind, the idea that women had intrinsic value stood religious culture on its head. In a society where might made right, the notion of leveraging strength to defend the defenseless was disruptive. But as you might imagine, this reshuffled value system was extraordinarily attractive to women.

Evolution Has Its Limits

As I stated earlier, society has changed. Women's rights have advanced. At least in some parts of the world. But men are the same. Otherwise, there would be no need for sexual harassment laws in the workplace. By now men should have adopted the Golden Rule as it relates to sexual expression: do unto women the way you want men to do unto your daughters and sisters. One doesn't need to be a theist to see the value in that.

Apparently, evolution has its limits. Men's propensity toward irresponsible, disrespectful, harmful sexual expressions has not diminished. While laws provide some protection, they fail to provide inspiration. Laws inform a man of how low he can go without a lawsuit. Laws do not prepare a man for a lifelong, healthy sexual relationship with a woman. That requires something more than a law. It requires a decision on the part of men, a decision to view and treat women differently. So guys, do you want to *become the person the person you are looking for is looking for?* Or are you content to get by with whatever you can with whomever will allow you to treat her that way? Are you ready to reach for what could be, or are you content to be led along by your evolutionary-dodging appetites and inclinations? Your answer to that question will determine your response to what I propose in the next chapter.

CHAPTER 7

THE WAY FORWARD

In case you took a week off after the last chapter, I'll recap. Gentlemen don't let their primordial impulses determine the way they treat women. They don't leverage gentlemen-like behavior to get what they want. Instead, gentlemen ascribe to every woman they meet the dignity due someone made in the image of God.

Every woman you're ever eyeball-to-eyeball with in the office, at a restaurant, in the gym, at school, or in the neighborhood, bears the image of God. Whether it's your wife's sister, the waitress, your kid's teacher, an office temp, or the teenage girl in the checkout lane at the grocery store—she deserves respect, honor, and consideration. This applies to the women you're attracted to and the women you're not attracted to. This is true for the women who flirt and text and chat and make it clear that they'd love to ... whatever ... and the women you went out with a couple of times but never called back. They all bear the image of God and, therefore, are worthy of honor. Imagine how much better and safer the world would be if every man adopted and adapted to this perspective.

Guys, just so you know, there's actually something in this for you. Every time you treat a woman with respect, you actually strengthen your self-control muscle. Every time you say no to your hit-her-with-a-club-and-drag-her-to-your-cave instinct, you're saying yes to self-control. Think of every proper response to a woman as a rep. The benefit to you is that when you meet the person you've been preparing for, you'll be prepared to treat her with the respect you believe she is due. To which most guys respond, "I don't need to practice self-control! When I meet the woman of my dreams, I'll step it up; I'll behave; I'll act right."

To which I respond: *No you won't.*

Here's why.

A caveman in a tux is still a caveman. Just because you left the cave doesn't mean the cave left you. Or me.

The Wedding Myth

Guys, you can't date like a slave owner, put on a tux, say "I do," and become a gentleman. Weddings don't change people. Weddings don't educate people. Weddings don't break bad habits. They break bank accounts but not habits. If you don't know how to treat a woman with respect before you say "I do," you'll be just as ignorant after the fact. If you aren't in the habit of treating women with respect before the vows, you won't treat 'em that way after the cake. And

I'm not just talking about the woman you carry across the threshold. I'm talking about the women she's going to catch you staring at during the reception. I know; I know; you would never do that. Truth is, you don't even know you're doing it! You haven't exercised those eye muscles in so long, they have a mind of their own. And no, that's not what sunglasses are for.

I've heard it dozens of times: "Andy, once I get married, all of that will change." But it doesn't. The only thing that changes at a wedding is a last name. Everything else remains the same, including your bad relational habits and your lack of self-control. A man may feel a different level of guilt about certain thoughts and habits after he's married. But guilt doesn't change a person. I'm a pastor. I know. I deal in guilt.

The "I'll change after the wedding" is nothing more than the male version of the myth we discussed throughout this book: *once I meet the right person, everything will be all right.* No it won't. That's not the way the world works. That's not the way *you* work. Guys, the best way to ensure that the chemistry leaves that highly chemical relationship you are looking so forward to is to ignore your self-control muscle until you say "I do."

You've been warned.

Old-Fashioned Is the New Fashion

With all that in mind, I want to make three suggestions.

They may seem old-fashioned. But remember, unbridled male passion predates old-fashioned by centuries. I want to begin by addressing your entertainment streams. Let's face it. Just about everything in the world of entertainment reinforces the notion that women are commodities. Culture is not going to teach you to or make it easy for you to honor women. At the same time, you're not going to abandon all forms of entertainment. But you can certainly abandon the streams of entertainment that go beyond suggestive to outright exploitive. You know the difference. Suggestive is what makes you feel uncomfortable when your mom walks into the room. Exploitive is when you feel compelled to tackle your mom before she sees what's on the screen.

Let's begin with your music. Men, if your playlist contains songs that refer to women as bitches and whores, you need to put this book down, find your mobile device, and start deleting. Now.

Seriously.

Right now.

"But Andy, do you know how much money I spent on all that music?"

Do you know how much money counseling and a divorce will cost you? Do you know how lonely, not to mention stupid, you're going to feel curled up on a couch at your friend's house with your MP3 player?

"But Andy, that terminology is cultural. It may be offensive, but I don't take it seriously."

I understand that argument. Here's why I don't buy it and you should quit trying to sell it. Words matter. Words are not only an expression of a culture; they shape culture. They have the power to direct culture. Let me illustrate.

Did you know the precursor to slavery, genocide, and racism is *always* a term or two used by an empowered group to dehumanize a specific segment of a population? If I can dehumanize you with an adjective, then eventually I will give myself permission to treat you like the adjective rather than a citizen of humanity. My family visited Rwanda several years ago. In preparation for our trip I immersed myself in stories associated with the genocide that ripped that nation apart in 1994. In the course of a hundred days, more than 800,000 Rwandans were murdered by Rwandans. Women suffered the most. They always do. In the months leading up to the official order that would begin the systematic slaughter, Hutu officials prepared a series of radio broadcasts wherein they listed all the supposed crimes of the Tutsi minority. These carefully worded messages were repeated day after day over loudspeakers set up in crowded sections of major cities. Leaflets were produced and distributed as well. Central to this heinous PR campaign was the dehumanizing of the Tutsi population. Tutsis were not citizens. Tutsis were not Rwandans. Tutsis were roaches. The message took hold. People find it difficult to harm another human being without provocation. But no one hesitates to kill a roach. When the killing began, neighbors butchered neighbors. Friends killed friends. Coworkers entered homes of people they had worked beside for years and committed murder with no initial sense of regret or remorse. They were simply ridding their nation and neighborhoods of a pestilence.

In Nazi Germany, Jews were called rats and Jewish women were repeatedly referred to as whores. Colonial

Americans had special names for American Indians as well as slaves. Yes, genocide, slavery, and racism are always accompanied by dehumanizing adjectives. If I can convince myself that you are less than human, I can treat you as such. Words matter. Labels are powerful. Adjectives are empowering. So do yourself and your future a favor and drop the derogatory adjectives. Especially toward women. Stop hiding behind and using culture as an excuse. A culture that degrades women is a culture that should be abandoned or changed, not defended. If you continue to entertain yourself with terminology that degrades women, you will eventually give yourself permission to treat them accordingly. Don't believe me? Just rewind to your last encounter with porn.

The Eyes Have It

Next up, one of the most powerful sources influencing our view of women: erotic imagery. Not porn. Erotic imagery. You know, the stuff you can access on Netflix and Amazon Instant Video. Most people think it's harmless. It's not. Here's why. Every time you intentionally entertain yourself with erotic images, you're at school. In this particular academy you're learning three very harmful lessons.

LESSON NUMBER ONE: One body isn't enough.
LESSON NUMBER TWO: A real body isn't enough.
LESSON NUMBER THREE: Your future wife's body won't
   be enough.

To which you may respond, "You can't say that; you've

never seen my future wife." Most guys think when they meet the *right* body, their need for *artificial* bodies will magically go away. It doesn't. In fact, in most cases, the desire for artificial bodies escalates. The result is a frustrated and disappointed groom. So what does the male consumer of artificial bodies do once he's married to an actual body? He subtly prods his real wife to try to match the eroticism of the make-believe ladies who've been entertaining him for years—ladies you would never dream of marrying because, after all, they're a bunch of whores and bitches. Not the marrying kind. At least not from the standpoint of the male consumer. Now, if you think I'm making this up or exaggerating, all you need to do is make an appointment with a local counselor and ask said counselor if the scenario I'm describing sounds familiar. What you'll quickly discover is that this is not a scenario the counselor hears occasionally, but weekly. Porn is job security for marriage counselors and divorce attorneys.

If you're interested in developing an actual romantic relationship with an actual woman, you need to drop out of the school of erotic imagery. That diploma pretty much ensures a life of romantic disappointment. Like most American men, you may be convinced that there's really no harm in looking at pictures and videos of naked women. Let me remind you, during World War II, the United States government gave the GIs as many cartons of cigarettes as they could carry. Why? Because smoking was a harmless pastime. For a while it was thought that smoking actually had health benefits! Lucky Strike and Phillip Morris used pictures of doctors in their ad campaigns. Phillip Morris ran an ad claiming their cigarettes cleared up throats irritated by other cigarette brands. But what do you know. Turns out cigarette smoking can kill you. Now it's hard to find a place to smoke in public. Several drugstores in our area have quit selling cigarettes entirely.

For decades, pastors and heads of organizations dedicated to the health of marriages and families have been saying porn is poison. Now there's overwhelming evidence to support those allegations. Turns out, porn has the power to change your brain. Don't believe me? Simply open your favorite browser and search "the effects of porn on the brain." If what you read scares you, it should. Internet porn does something to the male brain that Grandpa's *Playboy* magazine could only dream of. Internet porn takes advantage of the brain's neuroplasticity to create new pathways. This is what gives Internet porn its addictive quality. That's right, addictive quality. The more porn a man consumes, the more severe the changes to the brain. Consequently, the more difficult it is to close the browser and walk away.

You should know that no matter what your wife's body looks like, it will not have the brain-stimulating power of porn. If there's a competition, porn wins. Every time. Your attempts to get your wife or girlfriend to stimulate you the same way media stimulates you is futile. They're two entirely different things. You are dealing with different functions of the brain. This is why more and more men need porn as a stimulant for sex. One body doesn't do it for them. A real body doesn't do it for them. Their wives' bodies don't do it for them. And I'll let you in on a little secret. They WISH their wives' bodies were enough. In their efforts to experience the same high they find through porn, men crush the romance right out of their marriages. When a woman realizes nothing she does is enough, she will eventually give up. Who can blame her?

Porn is not a pastime. It's a pathway. Research confirms it. It's an addiction. It's a romance killer. It's a competition the woman you say you love will lose every time. Porn makes a promise it can't keep.

It promises to serve as a temporary, no-strings-attached substitute until a real woman comes along. The *right* woman. But in the end, porn erodes a man's ability to experience the very thing porn supposedly substitutes—a meaningful, satisfying, sexual relationship.

Awkward

Before we leave this uncomfortable topic, I want to make one last suggestion. Guys, if you plan to bring your erotic imagery pastime into what you hope will be a long-term relationship, either a marriage or otherwise, tell your partner up-front. Tell her the truth. Give her the option to choose whether she wants to compete with servers full of erotic imagery. Once you're sure she's the one, take her out for a nice, romantic dinner. During dessert, take her by the hand, look into her eyes, and say, "You know how I feel about you. You're the woman of my dreams. Because I feel the way I do about you, there's something I need to tell you that I've never told another woman. A real female body will never satisfy me. One female body will never satisfy me. Your body will never satisfy me. So while I'm sure sex will be enjoyable, it won't be enough to satisfy me. Just thought you should know."

You think I'm kidding, don't you? I'm not. You expect her to tell you about her credit card debt, don't you? After all, her financial issues become your issues if you get married. You expect her to tell you about her health issues, don't you? After all, she will expect you to be patient with whatever challenges they present. You expect her to tell you about any addictions or debilitating habits she's bringing into the relationship, don't you? So why wouldn't you tell her about your private pastime? Just tell her. Lower her expectations. No need for surprises during the first two or three months of your new life together. Besides, she's not a commodity. She's a person. She deserves the truth. If she chooses to move ahead with the relationship in spite of this revelation, more power to her. Either way, she deserves to know before she moves in or says, "I do." Give her the option to opt out beforehand rather than breaking her heart later.

Be honest. There are only two reasons you wouldn't tell her. Either you think a real body will free you from your private pastime, or you're afraid of her response. Hopefully by this point I've convinced you that "I do" doesn't magically empower anyone to do anything. So assuming that's not the reason, let's talk for a sentence or two about the "I'm afraid of how she will respond" excuse. While it's true that I don't know your girlfriend, I do know a thing or two about girls. If you're afraid of how she will respond *before* you limit her options with vows and a ring, you should be terrified of how she will respond to your secret *after* the caterer is paid and the band is on their way home. You may get a little credit for being transparent if you tell her up-front. But you ain't gonna get nothing but couch time if she discovers the truth later. You have something to fear either way. But the consequences of telling her up-front pale in comparison to the seismic eruption that will take place when she discovers your secret later. And she *will* discover it. Marriage has a way of uncovering singles' secrets. Carrying secrets into a long-term relationship of any type is a terrible idea.

Your best option, of course, is to accept erotic imagery for what it is and walk away. If that's difficult to do, then perhaps you should hit pause on your relationship until this habit is in the rearview mirror. You can't give yourself fully to *someone* else as long as you are mastered by *something* else. In this way, breaking the imagery habit is an important step in your quest to become the person the person you're looking for is looking for.

And that leads me to my final bit of advice for the men in the room.

Time Is Your Friend

If you've ever broken a bone or had invasive surgery you know how important the recovery process is. You also know what a hassle it is. Recovery takes time. Too much time. Everybody wants to skip rehab. Nobody wants to walk around in a sling. It's hard to stay off your feet. It's impossible to get anything done if you can't pick anything up. So what do we do? We lay low until we *feel* better. But feeling doesn't always signal healing. So we go back to work too soon. We start walking before the bone is completely healed. In some cases, our impatience prolongs the recovery process. In extreme cases, a second surgery is required.

If you've been gorging yourself on porn for the past several years, you need a recovery period. If you're a serial dater who equates dating with sex, you need a recovery period. Why? You may hate me for this. In your current state you are *incapable* of treating a woman with the respect she is due. Incapable. I'm not saying you don't know how. I'm suggesting you *can't* do it. Not for long, anyway. Your commoditizing thought patterns are too ingrained. Your behavioral patterns have worn deep ruts. Your mind just *goes there*, doesn't it? And promising and committing won't change any of that. Just as you can't promise and commit your sprained ankle back to health, you can't promise and commit your mind to purity. It takes time. You must keep the weight off and the ice on. There's no shortcut. Shortcuts lead to setbacks. You need time to heal.

So I want you to consider something. It's a bit radical. But if nothing else, it will give you an opportunity to recoup the money you lost when you deleted your playlist. I want you to consider taking an entire year off from all romantic pursuits. As in, set an alarm on your calendar and drop the terms *date, hook up, meet up, hang out, drop by, stay over, go out,* or *come by* from your vocabulary for 365 days. Time is your friend, especially if you use it wisely. By wisely, I mean use the time to renew your mind. Change your thinking. Regain a healthy, respectful view of women. Read. Subscribe to helpful podcasts. Develop a new group of friends. If you have a media addiction, use your year off to break it for good. Unsubscribe. Filter your Internet. Delete your watch list. Give away your television. Yes, you can live without a television. Besides, you have friends with televisions.

This is not a sacrifice. Porn and unhealthy serial dating are sacrifices. Taking a year off to break some bad habits and begin some new ones are investments. Your twelve-month romance sabbatical is an investment in your future. Better yet, these twelve months will give you time to become the person the person you're looking for is looking for. Borrowing the apostle Paul's language, your romance-free year will provide you with margin and motivation to "put away childish things." It will give you a chance to *grow up*, to become a gentleman.

You don't have to decide right now. Just think about it. I'll circle back around and ask you again in our last chapter together.

CHAPTER 8

THE TALK

So you know, this chapter is pretty much the *talk*. The one you should have had years ago with your parents. I imagine my version will differ considerably from theirs. Besides, theirs was probably ... not great. It lasted about ten or fifteen minutes and no one made eye contact. It was a bit like a trip to the dentist. Necessary and uncomfortable. Everybody was glad when it was over, and nobody learned a thing. There's not one kid in the history of kids who referred back to "the talk" when making a sexual decision. Not one. Besides, by the time most parents get around to having the talk, their kids have pretty much figured everything out. Or they think they have.

So for the next few pages I'm going to put on my parent hat and give you the scoop about sex. This is the stuff your parents didn't tell you and perhaps didn't know to tell you. By now you've had enough experience in this department to know there's no way a fifteen-minute talk during middle school can prepare anyone for the complexity of sexuality.

This sex talk revolves around one simple idea. It's something we all know intuitively. But it's something that never gets talked about. While that's unfortunate, it's understandable. This sexual reality isn't marketable. I don't think you could leverage it to sell stuff. It's not entertaining. I can't imagine turning it into a compelling plot. This sexual reality isn't all that sexy.

Enough drama.

Here it is.

Sex isn't just physical.

Sex is more than physical. Way more. Bet you knew that.

Western culture works hard to perpetuate the myth that sex is only physical. If it's consensual, safe, and you're protected against unwanted pregnancy, go for it. Kind of like, drink responsibly. Sex responsibly. Sex is a physical activity. It's the way we satisfy one of several physical appetites. Well, it's a way we *temporarily* satisfy a physical appetite. Either way, it's physical, and that's all there is to it. If there are no *physical* consequences, sex is pretty much inconsequential.

But you know better, don't you?

We all do.

Sex isn't *just* physical. There's more to sex because there's more to you. Unless you're a confirmed atheist, you would be quick to admit there's more to you than meets the eye. In fact, you don't want to be judged by what meets the eye alone, right? You're more than a body. You're a ... you. You have a heart, a soul, and a mind. There's an intangible component to you that you may not be able to define, but you would never deny. Any time you make a statement that includes the phrase "my body," you acknowledge there's more to you than a physical body. There's a *my* in there somewhere. As we're about to discover, and as perhaps you've already discovered, your sexuality is inexorably linked to the nonphysical part of you.

Here's how we know.

And this won't be fun.

Uncomfortably Obvious

Adults who were sexually abused as children find it difficult to heal and just *move on* with their lives. Why is that? Why, of all childhood experiences, is sexual abuse the one that gets shoved into the far recesses of a person's consciousness only to show up later at the most inopportune times? When it resurfaces, it's debilitating. But why? Why does childhood sexual abuse have so much power later in life? What's the big deal? It was so long ago. Why can't people just move on? Forgive and forget?

Those last two sentences are a bit hard to read, aren't they? They were hard to write. They're so callous. Nobody would respond that way to someone working through the pain and shame associated with childhood sexual abuse. But that's my point. If sex is just physical, then once any physical damage was healed, that would be the end of it. Granted, there may be some residual trust issues to work through. But every pastor, counselor, and victim knows the flood of emotions associated with sexual abuse goes way beyond trust issues. Kids report all kinds of things to their parents. But they rarely report sexual abuse. It's not on par with a playground brawl, an insensitive teacher, or even bullying. It cuts way deeper than any of those experiences.

Why is rape so much more devastating to a woman than being mugged or beaten up? Why is it easier for a woman to report assault than rape? What's the difference? They're both illegal. They're both physical. Why all the secrecy around rape? Report it, prosecute, and move on. Right?

No. Not right. There's a big difference between being roughed up or beaten up and being raped. But why? If sex is just physical, why the increased trauma associated with rape? I talked with a woman who was attacked in her home by an intruder. As he was preparing to rape her, she pleaded with him to stop. At the time she was living in a dangerous section of one of the most dangerous cities in the world, working with underprivileged children. She began telling her assailant what she did and why she was there, all the while begging him to leave. Miraculously, he did. The physical and emotional trauma she experienced that night landed her in the hospital for several days, followed by weeks of counseling. Eventually she moved back into the same neighborhood and resumed her work with kids. During her counseling she was told repeatedly how fortunate she was not to have been raped. While she knew that was true, she didn't fully understand the significance of her close call. Only later, as she interfaced with women who were not as fortunate did she truly understand what she had been delivered from. As terrifying as her ordeal had been, she was quick to acknowledge the vast contrasts between the consequences of rape and the threat of rape. But none of that surprises you, does it? There's something about being violated sexually that goes beyond a mere physical assault. Sex isn't just physical.

Through the years I've talked to dozens of men with sexual addictions—all kinds of sexual addictions. They all involved porn. Many of these men were into things that went way beyond a super-sized fascination with erotic imagery. Surprisingly, every man I've talked to who struggled with a sexual addiction was alienated from his father. Do I think that every man who is alienated from his father will end up with a sexual addiction? No. But I'm convinced there's a connection. I'm not alone. A forty-three-year-old porn addict who had just blown up his marriage after taking his sexual fantasies to another, unmentionable level, told me, "I'm convinced that if my dad hadn't run off, I wouldn't be in this condition." I asked him why he believed those dots were somehow connected. "I don't know," he said. "I don't blame my dad for my behavior. I just know I'm looking for something. The sex stuff is a substitute. I think I just miss my dad." While he didn't really connect the dots in a way either of us could explain, I think he was right. They are connected.

But what's the connection? How does not having a father in the home set up a man for an inordinate struggle with sexual temptation? Temptation that ultimately undermines the things that men say are important. Such as being there for their own sons and daughters. The men I've talked to would be quick to tell you their sexuality and their sexual struggles are not just physical. Something other than their male appetite for sex was driving their self-destructive behavior. Many of these men had given up on actual sex. It left them empty and unfulfilled. Yet their sexual appetite continued to control them. Sex is not just physical.

Something else I've noticed. Most people's greatest regrets involve something sexual. When anyone begins a conversation with, "I want to tell you something that I've never told anyone before," it's always sexual. It's never, "I was at the mall and I backed my car into the car across the parking lot and I didn't leave a note." Why is that? Why is there an unparalleled level of shame associated with inappropriate sexual behavior? Why do people carry sexual secrets so long?

Two more.

Why do husbands and wives feel so betrayed when their spouses have sex with someone else? Why does adultery divide a couple like nothing else? Think about the descriptive language we use. We say the offending party was "unfaithful." There's way more to marital faithfulness than reserving one's sexual activity for a spouse. But *faithful* is almost always synonymous with sexual faithfulness. Why is it so much easier to rescue a marriage when the betrayal is limited to an *emotional* affair? Most married people find it easier to forgive foreplay than intercourse. While even that is a form of betrayal, it's usually viewed as a significant step short of an actual affair. Most couples violate most of their wedding vows somewhere along the way. But sexual infidelity cuts far deeper than failing to consistently cherish, honor, and keep.

Last question.

Why were you so curious about the sexual history of the last person you dated? If you weren't, it may have been because you were hoping he or she wouldn't be too curious about yours. Jealousy related to previous relationships usually jumps exponentially when the previous relationships were sexual. But why? Who cares? Maybe you don't. But deep down, most of us do. We know. We know there's a big difference between dancing together and sleeping together. Both are physical. One is more than physical.

There's More

Sex isn't just one of several physical appetites. It's bigger than that. It runs deeper than that. It's not isolated to that. Our sexuality influences and informs every aspect of our lives. In some ways it mirrors the mystery of mind and brain. The intangible and the tangible. Sex is physical, but it's not *just* physical. If we forget, if we pretend not to notice, we pay. Perhaps worse, we make others pay. The previous paragraphs should make that abundantly clear.

Like all major decisions, sexual decisions follow us around. But while career, academic, and financial decisions dictate our future in visible and predictable ways, that's not always the case with decisions regarding our sexual expressions. If you've never been married, you should know the sexual decisions you make before you say "I do" will impact your sexual experience afterward. Your sexual experience will be impacted by your partner's pre-vow sexual decisions as well. What I can't adequately communicate in writing is how confusing this is for both parties when it happens. It's confusing because everybody knows something's wrong, but often neither party can put a finger on the exact problem. Like many of the illustrations I pointed to earlier, the dots don't always connect intuitively.

The "I" Word

There's a second important facet of sex we rarely hear about. This dimension is best captured in a term sometimes associated with the physical act of sex: *intimacy.* You may find this difficult to believe, but you have an appetite for intimacy. At the ideal end of the spectrum, intimacy involves knowing fully and being fully known. At some level, intimacy is what we're all looking for. Granted, it's not something everyone is actively looking for. When I teach this content with single men in the room, their body language says it all: *Andy, I'm not interested in intimacy. I'm interested in sex.* I get a different response from females. The thought of knowing someone fully and being fully known and accepted has an appeal that's often lost on us guys. But the appetite for intimacy is in us all. While we may not be *actively looking* for it, we are *inwardly longing* for it.

There's a significant and mysterious connection between one's sexual experience and one's capacity to experience relational intimacy. I'm tempted to retype that sentence several more times so you won't brush by it too quickly. This vital connection is completely ignored in our culture's celebration of sexual expression. Completely. The only place you will hear it discussed is in a counselor's office. People who make this connection in a counselor's office always wonder why no one ever explained it to them before. The fact that our culture not only ignores this connection but actually disses anyone who suggests sexual moderation is the reason I felt compelled to write this book. Our refusal to acknowledge the obvious reminds me of Hans Christian Andersen's tale, *The Emperor's New Clothes.*

No one close to the Emperor would acknowledge what was obvious to everyone for fear of being considered unfit to serve in the upper echelon of the kingdom. When he paraded through the city streets, the peasants took their cue from the upper class and ooohed and ahhhhed as he walked by ... in his underwear. Everyone pretended because everyone felt pressured to pretend. But everyone knew.

> Nobody would confess that he couldn't see anything, for that would prove him either unfit for his position, or a fool. No costume the Emperor had worn before was ever such a complete success.

Finally a child, someone too young to be caught up in the civic insanity, blurted out what was obvious to everyone:

> "But he hasn't got anything on."

Remember what happened next?

> "Did you ever hear such innocent prattle?" said its father. And one person whispered to another what the child had said, "He hasn't anything on. A child says he

hasn't anything on." "But he hasn't got anything on!" the whole town cried out at last.

The Emperor shivered, for he suspected they were right. But he thought, "This procession has got to go on." So he walked more proudly than ever, as his noblemen held high the train that wasn't there at all.

I don't assume a book, particularly a book written by a middle-aged pastor, will send shock waves of realization through our culture. I'm not sure anything can. But if I had to place a bet on where I believe our best hope for a revival of sexual sanity rests, I would bet on a future generation. A generation that refuses to pretend. A generation willing to declare what every generation has always known. Sex isn't just physical. To treat it as if it were is to undermine one's capacity for what we all long for. Intimacy.

Inexorably Linked

Your potential for relational intimacy is inexorably linked to your sexual experience. Like learning to change a flat tire, nobody is all that interested in understanding this relationship until there's a problem. Then the response is almost always universal. "Why didn't someone explain this to me when I was younger?" If you have any doubts about this important connection, all you need to do is talk with an adult who is coming to terms with childhood sexual abuse. If you have sexual abuse in your background, you know. What's often overlooked or ignored, however, is that just as

unwanted sexual experience impacts one's ability to expe
rience intimacy later in life, a string of consensual sexual
experiences can have a similar effect; some would argue the
same effect. The heartbreaking consequence of our sexually
liberated culture is that single men and women are undermining their own potential for sexual fulfillment later in life.
By divorcing sexual expressions from relational permanency
they are — perhaps you are — damaging their potential for
intimacy. The battle for intimacy that victims of sexual abuse
are forced to fight is the battle that those who see no problem with casual sex are choosing to have to fight. While that
may sound like hyperbole, it's not. If you were the victim of
childhood sexual abuse, I would imagine that feels like an
unfair comparison. In terms of experience, it certainly is. In
terms of outcome, it's not. Because sex isn't just physical.

I'm not railing against our culture's approach to all things
sexual because I'm anti-sex or even anti-you-having-sex.
Quite the contrary. I'm for it. But I'm for all of it. The nonphysical component as well as the physical one. More importantly, I'm for you. I'm for you experiencing the richest,
most rewarding sexual experience possible. That may require
a shift in your thinking, which leads to some countercultural
changes in behavior. But in the end, you win.

Here's why.

Eventually

At some point you hope to settle down. When you do,
you'll want the sexual part of your settled-downness to be

rich. Fun. Fulfilling. Right? Someday you hope to be in a relationship that's sexual but more than sexual. What you want, whether you like this term or not, is intimacy. Oneness. Friendship laced with sexual passion. Or perhaps the other way around. Either way, you're hoping for a sexual *relationship*, not just sex. Problem is, non-relational sexual experiences combined with short-term relational sexual experiences have the potential to diminish the significance of sex in that once-in-a-lifetime relationship you're hoping for. Sex outside the context of a committed long-term relationship undermines the significance of sex within the relationship you will someday value most. That should concern you. As sexual encounters increase, your potential to experience sexual intimacy decreases. Consequently, you undermine your own future sexual fulfillment; you damage or diminish your own capacity for intimacy. Divorcing sex from a committed relationship ultimately diminishes the significance of sex within a committed relationship. If you were *just* a body, that may not be the case. If sex were purely physical, that may not be the case. But you are more than a body and sex is more than physical.

Not Safe

For these reasons and more, I don't love the phrase "safe sex." I understand the necessity of a physical first line of defense against STDs and unwanted pregnancies. But the adjective *safe* is misleading. I've talked to too many men and women whose *safe sex* habits left them empty and detached, in some cases unable to connect with their spouses sexually in anything other than a perfunctory way. What is touted as *safe* for the body is *dangerous* for the soul. While your body is designed with the capacity to successfully accommodate multiple sex partners with no apparent consequences, *you* are not. Sex was given as an expression of physical oneness designed to mirror relational permanence. When that which was designed to amplify oneness isn't reserved for one, its significance is diminished.

History

It's a mistake to play fast and loose with your sexuality assuming that when you finally meet the right person, your sexual history and hers will be just that ... history. It doesn't work that way. We aren't *designed* to work that way. Our sexual histories are always a memory or two away. They raise their ugly and sometimes not-so-ugly heads at the most inopportune and inappropriate times. Often, during sex with the *right* person. Memories. Ghosts. Guilt. Comparison. Fear of comparison. The more sexually active people were before they met the *right person*, the more inclined they are to lie about their sexual histories. Sandra and I recently talked to a newlywed whose husband had just confessed to sleeping with more than twenty prostitutes during his late teens and twenties. Extreme, you say? The more extreme the story, the less likely it is to surface before an unsuspecting *right person* has the opportunity to say, "Since you did, I don't."

I know somebody out there is thinking, *But what about*

forgiveness? Shouldn't I just forgive? Shouldn't I be forgiven? Yes. But forgiveness and consequences are two entirely different things. I can forgive you for backing into my car, but that does nothing to address the damage you caused. I've talked to countless individuals who reserved sex for marriage but whose husbands or wives had not. They were encouraged to forgive their soon-to-be-spouses for not *waiting*. Which they did. But the consequences remained. When a guy is unable to give himself wholly to his wife because he has given himself away to other women, there will be some bumps, tears, resentment, and anger. While most couples push through, the avoidable tragedy is they are forced to do so when the relationship is new. While one's sexual past can be forgiven, it is never completely forgotten.

I don't live in a cave. I'm aware that fewer and fewer people are *saving themselves* for marriage. Over 30 percent of the couples that come to us for premarital counseling are already living together. Of the remaining 70 percent, most are already involved sexually. You might assume couples who are living and sleeping together have worked through the sexual challenges created by their sexual histories. Not so. In fact, many couples use their time with our premarital mentors to air their frustrations and concerns regarding those very issues.

Sexual involvement early in a relationship masks relational issues. But eventually they surface and often diminish or kill sexual passion. Relationship problems have a way of doing that. Without warning, a couple whose sexual chemistry drove the relationship forward find themselves drifting listlessly. Before long they start looking for someone to blame. They rarely look in the mirror.

For this reason we require couples involved sexually to curtail sleeping together during premarital counseling. Those living together we ask to separate until after the wedding. When necessary, we help facilitate alternative living arrangements. While this is never convenient, it's always helpful. Hitting the pause button sexually makes it easier to surface and talk about relational challenges hovering below the surface. Again, nothing masks relational dysfunction like sexual involvement. Asking a couple to curtail sex for the sake of the relationship rarely makes sense in the moment. Those who comply thank us later. And only 7 percent call off the wedding.

Turning Off

Before we move on, I would be remiss not to mention one more potential surprise for sexually active couples planning to marry. It's beyond my pay grade to explain why the following happens, but it's such a common occurrence that counselors and psychologists have names for it. Sexually active women often shut down sexually once they're married. There are interesting if not complicated explanations for this syndrome. Understanding it doesn't seem to help. The results are devastating. I've heard it so many times I've lost count: "Before we were married, she couldn't keep her hands off of me. She was an animal. But a couple years in, it's like somebody threw a switch. She's not interested in sex.

At least not with me." Men feel tricked. Seduced. Confused. Eventually they get angry. Understandably so. To add to the confusion, the women in these scenarios are rarely bothered at all by the change. For them it's quite simple. They just aren't interested in sex with their husbands. That's all there is to it. Since they don't miss it, it's really not a problem ... other than fending off his unwanted passes. In the cases I've dealt with, they're content to be roommates and wonder why their husbands can't just *love them the way they are*. On those occasions when a husband can get his wife to see a counselor, the women in these scenarios usually blame their lack of interest on their husbands.

- "He's too fat."
- "He's too demanding."
- "It's all he thinks about."
- "I feel pressured."
- "I've lost respect."

I've seen men go to extremes to address everything on the complaint list. I've never known it to make a bit of difference. At the same time, I've never talked to a disinterested wife who I sensed wasn't being honest. In most instances, they really weren't sure *why* they lost interest. The to-do lists they gave their husbands were generally an attempt to come up with something to explain their admitted lack of passion.

These scenarios usually end the same way. After years of conflict somebody finds an available shoulder to cry on. Oddly enough, it's just as likely to be the wife as the husband. Often, an old boyfriend who's hit a rough patch in his marriage as well. Eventually somebody hires an attorney and the entire thing ends badly. But once the dust settles ... in some cases before the dust settles ... both parties are on the hunt for the next *right person.*

Sex is physical, but it's more than physical. Your sexual experiences affect your capacity for intimacy. Sexual purity isn't an idea whose time has come and gone. Sexual purity is a strategy. It's an investment in your happiness and the happiness of your future partner. Why? Because purity *now* paves the way to intimacy *later.*

It's Complicated

One of the most memorable conversations I've had on the subject of sex and singleness took place early in my career while I was working for my dad. From time to time he would invite me to preach in his absence. On one such occasion I made an off-the-cuff remark about teenagers and abstinence. The next day a woman called my office and asked to meet with me ASAP. Something I said in my message confused her and she needed clarification. A week or so later I found myself sitting across the table from an attractive, sophisticated, serious, thirty-something woman. She was all business. As soon as she sat down, she stated her reason for coming to see me: "So, Andy, in your sermon you said sex was for married people. But that only applies to teenagers, right? And don't get me wrong; I think that's good advice for teenagers. But that rule doesn't apply to ..." she paused, "to people in my situation. You know, older people who've been married before. Does it?"

Her directness was a bit intimidating. Heck, she was a bit intimidating. While I found myself at a loss for words, I started talking anyway. Normally not a good idea. But what came out of my mouth was so profound I've never forgotten it. In fact, after she left, I wrote it down. I heard myself ask, "Well, let me ask you a personal question: Has sex as a single woman made your life better or more complicated?" If she had answered, "Better," I'm not sure where I would have gone from there. Probably home. But she didn't. Instead she teared up. She went from intimidating, self-assured professional to a young woman whose heart had suddenly been exposed. "Complicated," she said, "definitely complicated." Then I asked a question I've asked a thousand times since. "If God is a heavenly Father who loves you and wants the best for you ... and he knows sex apart from marriage will complicate your life ... what would you expect him to say about it?" She looked away and was quiet for a moment. Then she nodded and said, "I get it. The rules apply to people like me. Of course they do. Thank you."

Crisis averted.

Several months later, we crossed paths again. Big smile. None of the hardness I encountered in our first meeting. She was with friends. But I couldn't resist. "So, how are things?" I asked. "Different for sure," she said. "Good different?" I asked. "Yes, good different," she said. "Not so complicated."

Good Different

So, what about you? Better or complicated? Maybe both. If you knew then what you know now, perhaps you would have been more discerning and less available. While you can't *go* back, it's imperative that you *look* back. Looking back is mandatory if you plan to move forward. Mandatory but scary. Admitting to yourself that you've been irresponsible sexually may be the most frightening admission of your life. Here's why. If you've been in a series of sexual relationships, you've developed a habit you're probably unaware of. After each breakup or one-time tryst, you've forced yourself to just move on. You had to. But you did something else as well. You told yourself it didn't matter. But it did. You lied to yourself. You didn't let yourself feel what you should have felt. It would have been overwhelming. Every time you *moved on*, you added one more layer of protection around your heart. That's why, to quote an old Rod Stewart song, "The first cut is the deepest." What you felt after that first sexual relationship ended is a level of regret you've probably never felt since. There's a reason. Your heart was harder the second time around.

Guys, this applies to us as well. In your case, perhaps you lied and promised and said, "I love you." You said whatever you needed to say to get your way. Then, when you were ready, you walked away. In your own callous fashion you justified it. But the fact that you justified it underscores that it wasn't *just*. It wasn't right. You would be tempted to kill a guy who treated your little sister that way. So you shoved those feelings down deep. The guilt would have been unbearable. Worse, the guilt would have forced you to behave differently.

If you've been in a series of sexual relationships, you have unknowingly and unintentionally uncoupled sex from your soul. This is why it's begun to mean less and less. It's expected but not all that special. This is one reason sexually active singles develop a hard exterior. All regret is difficult to live with. Sexual regret may be the most difficult. So we lie to ourselves. We tell ourselves we haven't done anything wrong. It was his fault. Her fault. You were young. You were drunk. All of which may be true. But you're still guilty. Nobody wants to feel guilty. So we create narratives we can live with and move on. Or attempt to.

The moment you decide to acknowledge your error, to use a religious term, "your sin," your heart and your past will reconnect and the flood of emotion that follows may be overwhelming. Understandably so. You've been storing up stuff. If there's something in you that fears what you may feel if you were to stop and face your sexual history, all the more reason to do so. Reconnecting your heart to your past is essential if you're going to become healthy. It will prepare you to commit. Being honest about and taking responsibility for your past is a necessary step toward *becoming the person the person you're looking for is looking for.*

As I've read and reread this chapter, I know how difficult this content will be for many. If you've stayed with me this far, I imagine you are looking for *different*. Good different. If that's the case, have yourself a good cry and keep reading.

CHAPTER 9

DESIGNER SEX

Christians believe the mysterious link between sex and intimacy is the result of *divine design*. Think about it. It took something or someone with extraordinary relational capacity and imagination to design the human sexual experience. I don't think evolution is that smart or relationally savvy. Christians believe God added the relational dynamic to the sexual equation on purpose, for a purpose. While the procreative purpose of sex is reflected in the entire animal kingdom, relational intimacy, as experienced through sexual intercourse, looks to be a gift reserved for the human race. Christians aren't the only group that acknowledges there's more to sex than making babies. Culture certainly celebrates and elevates the pleasure side of the equation. But Christians believe the significance of sex goes beyond babies and bliss.

Jesus associated sex with the start of a new and permanent family unit. According to Jesus, sex symbolizes the knitting together of two people to form a new entity.[8] While Jesus never used the term *intimacy*, he made a statement that carries all the weight of that word plus some. During a dispute with religious leaders over the question of when it was appropriate for a man to divorce his wife, Jesus cited an Old Testament statement and then added a few words of his own:

> " 'For this reason a man will leave his father and mother and be united to his wife, and the two will become one flesh.' So they are no longer two, but one flesh. Therefore what God has joined together, let no one separate."
>
> (MATTHEW 19:5–6)

Think about this phrase for a moment: "So they are no longer two, but one flesh." There's something magical and mystical, even romantic, about that. No longer two, but one. Through marriage, something that didn't exist before comes to be. Within the context of this mysterious disappearing trick, sex finds its proper, God-designed context. Sex is for married people because sex is a physical expression of relational oneness—permanence. You can make babies with a lot of people. Sex can be pleasurable with a lot of people. But you can only be one with one other person. If relational *oneness* is something you hope to experience, then save sex for the person with whom you want to become one. Reserve your body for the one for whom you are reserving that unique commitment. Give your body to the person to whom you pledge your life. To do otherwise is to diminish the significance of sex with that "I've waited all my life for you" person. Because you didn't.

Long Ago and Far Away

As we discovered earlier, twenty or so years after Jesus, the apostle Paul came along and contextualized Jesus' teaching for a predominantly non-Jewish audience, an audience whose sexual ethic paralleled much of what we find in contemporary culture, only worse. In the first-century Gentile world, sex was all about sensual pleasure and women were considered commodities. Nothing new there. In the first century, prostitution was not only legal, it was encouraged. While it was considered immoral for a man to have sex with another man's wife, sex with prostitutes was not. Marcus Tullius Cicero, a Roman philosopher, lawyer, and orator, reflected the mood of his day when he wrote:

> If anyone there thinks that young men should be forbidden association even with prostitutes, he is certainly very stern; but he is also in disagreement not only with the permissiveness of this century, but even with the custom and indulgences of our ancestors.[9]

Prostitutes were not the only legitimate vehicle for extramarital activity. Slaves were used and abused sexually as a matter of course. While it was a criminal offense to have sex with another man or woman's slave, what slave owners did with their own slaves was their business. Pederasty was legal as long as it involved slaves or non-citizens and as long as a Roman male did not play a passive role. Male passivity of any sort was viewed as weakness. Having sex with young boys was not.

So, if you think the sexual ethic I'm advocating in this book seems a bit behind the times in our culture, imagine the challenge of introducing this message to the first-century cities of Ephesus, Corinth, and Rome. Yet everywhere he went, Paul found pockets of people who were receptive to his instruction regarding sexual purity. They saw Paul's message for what it was: a way of life that restored dignity to women and self-respect to men. It was life giving. Liberating. Leveraging his Jewish values along with the teaching of Jesus, Paul taught that sex was more than simply an appetite to be filled with whomever could be coerced or paid to participate. According to Paul, sex was designed to reflect and illustrate relational oneness. This was God's divine design.

Like Nothing Else

Paul's letter to the Christians in Corinth contains his most straightforward teaching on this topic. It also contains a profound insight regarding the importance of sexual purity. Here's what he wrote:

> Flee from sexual immorality. All other sins a person commits are outside the body, but whoever sins sexually, sins against their own body.
>
> (1 CORINTHIANS 6:18)

His first statement sounds rather preacher-esque. But unlike most preachers, Paul actually gave a reason to support his instruction. Not the reason his audience, then or now, would expect. He didn't go parental and say, "Flee immorality because I said so." He didn't go sex-ed and say, "Flee immorality to avoid an STD or a baby you can't take care of." Most surprisingly he didn't go Sunday-school with, "Flee immorality because sex is for married people."

Without looking back, and please play along, can you recall *why* Paul says to flee immorality? Don't look! Most people can't. Most people who grew up in church can't. Not yet! Chances are you've either heard or been taught your entire life that the Bible teaches against premarital sex. It does. But chances are no one told you *why* the New Testament urges believers to reserve sex for marriage. Here's a shocker. The *why* has nothing to do with disease or unwanted pregnancy. You may be interested to know that the Bible does not say the primary, much less the exclusive, purpose of sex is to make babies. Biblical authors do not condemn sexual pleasure. God's not worried about us having too much fun.

So why all the fuss?

Why would Paul instruct his Christian audience to "flee" from immorality?

Here's why:

All other sins a person commits ...

Sexual sin is like no other sin. Paul puts sexual sin in a category all by itself. "All other sins ..." Here's the second part:

All other sins a person commits are outside the body, but whoever sins sexually, sins against their own body.

Two thousand years ago Paul warned us of the very thing

our contemporary culture discovers the hard way. When we sin sexually, we hurt *ourselves*. But not physically. Paul's primary concern is not the physical consequences of sex. Apparently he chose to leave that topic to the sex-ed teachers. Paul's concern falls into the realm of what we discussed in the previous chapter. In two sentences he says what it took me the entire previous chapter to explain. When we ignore God's *relational* purpose for sex ... when we rip sex out of its divinely designed relational context ... we hurt ourselves. Even when there are no physical consequences, we hurt ourselves.

After all, sex is not just physical. Sexual sin is like no other sin because your sexuality bridges body and soul. Sex is a physical act that reaches beyond your physical body. Sexual sin is like no other sin because it cuts deeper than other sin. It leaves a more noticeable scar. When you sin sexually, you literally sin against your true *self*. Your soul self. To sin against yourself is essentially to betray and steal from yourself. Sexual sin robs you of your own future. Sexual sin undermines future intimacy. Sexual sin creates an obstacle to honesty. Sexual sin is the sin we will be most tempted to hide, the sin we will most likely try to smuggle into future relationships. Sexual sin eventually equates to self-inflicted pain. I could go on and on. So yeah, the New Testament teaches that sex is for married people. Not because God is against sex, but because God is for YOU. God, who created sex and created sex for you, is for you. So of course God has something to say on this important topic.

Paul didn't say sexual sin is unlike any other sin because

God thinks less of sexual sinners than other kinds of sinners. Somebody at your church may feel that way but not your heavenly Father. You won't find that in the New Testament. Paul didn't say sexual sin is unlike any other sin because God won't forgive it. On the contrary, Jesus rescued a woman caught in adultery from being stoned, telling all the good people to go away and leave her alone. Then he looked her in the eye and said what he would say to all sexual sinners if they were to give him the opportunity:

"Then neither do I condemn you ... Go now and leave your life of sin."

(JOHN 8:11)

Sexual sin is not unforgivable, but it can make life unbearable. Sexual sin won't send you to hell, but it has the potential to make your life hell on earth. There's nothing like sex. So Paul reminds us there's nothing like sexual sin. The beauty and magnificence of sex is mirrored by the pain and complexity it can bring when taken out of its divinely designed context.

Unite

Earlier in this same section of Scripture, Paul reiterated the relational component of sex with a rather unusual question:

Do you not know that he who unites himself with a prostitute is one with her body? For it is said, "The two will become one flesh."

(1 CORINTHIANS 6:16)

This is a jab. "Do you not know?" Implication: "Doesn't everybody know?" His concern wasn't the legality of prostitution but the implications of sex outside of a committed relationship. To paraphrase, "Hey gang, did you know that your recreational sexual encounters have long-term relational implications?" When Paul's first-century audience read this, they must have thought, *Wait a minute, nobody's* **uniting**. *We aren't becoming* **one**. *We're just having sex. I don't remember her name and I didn't bother giving her mine.*

But Paul chose his words carefully. The Greek term translated *unites* in our English Bibles carries the idea of permanency, bonding. Implication: a one-night or one-weekend fling is a bonding experience. Then, to everybody's surprise, he referenced the Old Testament "one flesh" concept. To which his Jewish audience must have thought, *Hang on, that's code for starting a family. I thought you were warning us about sex with prostitutes.*

I belabor this point because, like Paul's culture, our culture has embraced the notion that *what we do now with our bodies sexually has no correlation to what we hope to experience relationally later.* Everybody assumes the past is the past. Just burn those old letters, tear up those old pictures, erase your Facebook page, and move on. Which is fine if you're talking about a career change. But it doesn't work that way in the arena of romance and relationships. You know that and we've covered that. So why do we fight so hard to ignore that thing in us that whispers, "You're going to regret this"?

Two thousand years ago—think about that—two thousand years ago, Paul warned his sexually free audience that sex was designed as an adhesive. It's sticky, meant to help hold two people together permanently. Thus the term *unites*. Sex has a uniting quality. If you apply, remove, reapply, and re-remove an adhesive, it begins to lose its adhesiveness. As difficult as this may be for you to accept, the same thing happens sexually. Every time you have sex with a different partner, you apply, remove, then reapply this powerful but somewhat fragile relational uniter. Eventually your sexual experience will begin to lose its *stickiness*. The way you'll know is because sex will begin to lose its *significance*.

Flipped

Guys, if sex is an assumed part of your dating regimen, you know this to be the case. Some sex is better than other sex, isn't it? Think about that. You've successfully isolated sex from intimacy. Now it's almost purely physical. Isn't it interesting that you no longer evaluate the quality of your sexual experiences by the quality of the relationship? In fact, it's the other way around, isn't it? You evaluate the quality of the relationship by the quality of the sex. Good sex, good relationship. Bad sex, time to move on. She was good in bed, so you asked her out again. Think about that. It hasn't always been that way, has it? Something changed. So while I'm meddling, let me make a prediction. You will be tempted to marry the girl who provides you with the best sexual experience. It happens all the time. But once you're married, you'll be expected to have a ... relationship! But she may not be very good at that. You may not be good at it either.

Again, sex before marriage covers a multitude of relational inadequacies. As the relationship sours, guess what else takes a hit? You'll begin wondering, *What's wrong with her? What happened to the fun, spontaneous, sexual creature I married or moved in with?* Then your mind will wander back to those other fun, spontaneous sexual creatures from the past. That's when Facebook becomes your friend.

When sex becomes a tool for evaluating relational compatibility, you are in a dangerous place. You are upside down. Your chances for long-term relational success are close to zero. Zero. And ... you did it to yourself. Sexual sin is unlike any other sin. Sexual sin enables wonderful people to undermine their own futures. Sex is an easy substitute for relationship. But in the end, the sex is no better than the relationship. If sex is casual, you will have a difficult time making it meaningful. Even in your most meaningful relationships. If these last few paragraphs describe you, and you hope someday to enjoy a permanent, pleasurable relationship, you have some work to do. And I'll suggest some next steps in the following chapter.

No Thanks

You may be tempted to brush all this off with, "Andy, thanks for your opinion, but everybody's different. Not everybody's religious like you. When it comes to something as personal as sex, people have to decide for themselves." Before you go there, let me make one observation. If sex were like art or music, you would be right. If sex and sexuality were simply a matter of personal taste, you would have a good argument. But they're not. Music and art don't create outcomes. Music and art don't have consequences. Music and art are not part of a cause-and-effect equation.

Sex is like nutrition. Regardless of your taste and preferences, nutritional principles determine the outcome of what you eat. You may prefer dairy products over wheat products, but if you consume too much of either, the outcome is pretty much the same. Like you, I've seen overweight people coming out of Mexican restaurants, Italian restaurants, and fast food restaurants. And I've seen fit people walk out of all three as well. It's not taste that makes the difference. It's consumption. The laws of consumption apply to everybody. Know why? Because our bodies share a similar design.

Our bodies share a similar design when it comes to our sexuality as well. God designed your sexuality to be expressed within a specific context. You can choose to express your sexuality outside the parameters of that divine design. But you can't choose the outcome. If you're like most people, you'll do everything in your power to *control* the outcome. But eventually you will lose that battle as well. Perhaps you've experienced the futility of trying to control outcomes. Perhaps that's why you chose to read this book.

Let's Be Honest

If you find the whole *uniting, becoming one, sticky* thing to be a bit over the top, that's understandable. Nobody's singing or making movies about it. But before you dismiss it, I want to draw your attention to something you know intuitively. Something in your soul that you didn't put there that underscores the truth of what Jesus and Paul taught us so long ago.

Romance is fueled by exclusivity.

The essence of romance is discovering that the sole object of your affection has chosen you to be the sole object of his or her affection as well. Does anyone dream of hearing, "I love you with *most* of my heart"? Or, "I can't stop thinking about you *and* your roommate"? How about, "I want to spend the rest of my thirties with you"? When it comes to romance, anything short of exclusivity doesn't feel right. Or at least it shouldn't. I love the lyrics of Safety Suit's song "Never Stop." The first verse especially, which pledges "let every woman know I'm yours" and "you're the only one I see" kind of exclusivity.

Guys, isn't that the way you hope to feel about somebody someday? Ladies, isn't that what you're looking for? Hoping for? Isn't *exclusivity* the thing that makes a love story a love story? Exclusivity happens when you give yourself wholly to the one person who is willing to give him- or herself wholly to you. So maybe all that uniting and oneness and stickiness language isn't so far-fetched after all. Perhaps the thing you long for is the thing God created you for. And perhaps what on the surface seems so prohibitive is actually God's way of protecting you for the very thing you one day hope to experience.

This is why "practice makes perfect" doesn't apply to sex. This is why practice undermines the essence of romance. Sex with multiple partners diminishes the potential for exclusivity, and thus the potential for intimacy. This is just one more reason most sexually active people lie about their sexual histories when they meet their *one and onlys*. They know—we know—intuitively, that multiple sexual experiences conflict with exclusivity. While writing these last two chapters, I've had two heartbreaking conversations with women whose husbands recently confessed the extent of their premarital sexual escapades. In both cases their husbands confessed to a "couple" of sexual relationships when they were "younger." Eventually the truth came out. Neither man had any idea how many women they'd slept with. Their wives are devastated.

Your sexual experiences before marriage may enhance your sexual experience once you're married, but they won't enhance your relationship. Just the opposite. Romance is fueled by exclusivity, not experience. Sex is not like learning to play the violin. If you want to learn to play the violin, you'll need lessons and a lot of practice. People have been figuring out sex on their own for millenniums.

The Story of Your Life

I've been teaching on this topic long enough to know how hopeless and condemned these last two chapters will leave many of my readers. Every time I speak on this topic, someone says, "Andy, I wish I'd heard this when I was eighteen." The unspoken message is, *I think it's too late for me.* If that's you ... if you had to reach for a tissue during these last two chapters ... if you had to close the book and walk around the room ... if you closed the book and threw it across the room ... if you're mad at me, mad at you, just plain mad ... I have some good news. And I swear (which I rarely do) I'm not just tacking this on to make you feel better. The good news is you get to *decide* your way forward. Specifically, you get to *decide* what story you will tell three or four years from now. Every event in your past is part of your story. We all have some chapters we hope nobody reads. Today you will make another entry in the story that is your life. Tomorrow, today's entry will simply be part of your story. So here's the question I would like for you to wrestle with before moving on to the final chapter:

What story do you want to tell?

Your response to what you've just read is about to become part of your story. What story do you want to tell? In the final chapter I'm going to challenge you to do something I've been challenging people to do for years. Many men and women have taken me up on this unusual challenge and written to thank me. But their decisions to follow through were predicated on their answers to this question: Three years from now, when you are looking back on the past three years, what story do you want to tell?

Odds are you don't want to fill the next three years with events you'll be tempted to lie about when you meet someone special. If past decisions have left you with regret, guilt, and perhaps shame, I doubt you want any more of those feelings in your story. So, what story *do* you want to tell? Regardless of what you do with what you've read here, you will continue writing the story of your life. Hopefully, you will fall in love. Just as you will want to know that person's story, he or she will want to know yours. What story do you want to tell?

If your initial response is, "Quit asking me that! I don't want to tell my story. I don't want anyone to know my story. I have a bad story," that's all the more reason to ask the question. Here's why. If you don't decide what story you want to tell, you will continue with your current story. *Feeling bad rarely results in doing better.* Knowing better and doing better are two separate things. Guilt and regret usually drive people toward behaviors that result in more guilt and more regret. Face it. If guilt were enough to change a person's behavior, the Catholic church would be full of perfect people and Baptist churches wouldn't be far behind. I grew up in a wonderful Baptist church. I knew exactly what I was supposed to do. When I didn't do it, I felt guilty. So I confessed my sin and went right back out and did it again. What's *it*, you ask? That's my story! I'd rather talk about yours.

People don't give up what they're currently doing until they're convinced that what they're currently doing is an obstacle to where or who they want to be. People change when they have a picture of a preferred future. No matter how bad you feel about your past ... regardless of the consequences associated with your behavior ... ain't nothing going to change until you *decide* what story you want to tell two or three years from now. If you don't decide, your story will go something like this:

> *After my first sexual experience, I pretty much decided sex was just part of the deal. I assumed I would eventually*

settle down with somebody. But I didn't see any harm in fooling around until I met the right person. Who doesn't? Then a friend recommended a book. I read it. The author beat me up pretty bad. Told me I needed to prepare to commit. Told me my sexual history was going to undermine intimacy later on. He kept saying I needed to become somebody rather than just look for somebody. It made sense. And I might have taken him more seriously if I were twenty. But I wasn't. So, I just kept looking for the right person and enjoying myself along the way. If I'm honest, I hope to meet somebody whose sexual history is a bit less interesting than mine. And yeah, I'll probably keep most of mine to myself. In spite of what the guy who wrote the book said, once I meet the right person, I'm confident everything will be all right.

That's one option. Here's another one:

After my first sexual experience, I pretty much decided sex was just part of the deal. I assumed I would eventually settle down with somebody. But I didn't see any harm in fooling around until I met the right person. Who doesn't? Then a friend recommended a book. I read it. The author beat me up pretty bad. Told me I needed to prepare to commit. Told me my sexual history was going to undermine intimacy later on. He kept saying I needed to become somebody rather than just looking for somebody. It made sense.

I tried to put it down a couple times and just move on with my life. But I knew he was right. I was tempted to use my age and sexual experience as an excuse. You know, if I'd heard that earlier maybe I would have done things differently. But at the end, he reminded me that my future does not have to be a continuation of my past. I was honest with myself. My recent past was not a story I would be proud to tell. Especially to someone I was in love with. He was right. I would probably lie about my past. So I decided to begin writing a better story. I took a break from looking for the right person and focused on becoming the right person. I decided to prepare to commit. As part of that preparation, I decided that from that moment on, I would reserve sex for marriage. That was three years ago. I'm a different person today.

Which story do you want to tell?
Better question.
Which story would you prefer to hear?
That should tell you something.

CHAPTER 10

IF I WERE YOU

If you're a high school student whose parents are paying you to read this book, you can skip ahead to the conclusion and collect your cash. If this book is a rehash of what you already know, believe, and embrace as a lifestyle, you may skim your way on over to the conclusion as well. I'm sorry there's no cash prize for you. However, there's always eBay. For everybody else, deep breath. We're almost done.

As I mentioned in the introduction, I pastor a network of churches attracting thousands of students and singles. Our environments and worship services are designed with seekers, starters, and returners in mind. When I address the subjects of sex, marriage, and relationships, which I do often, I assume that the values, habits, and backgrounds of my audience mirror the values and culture of our city. So for years I've challenged singles and students to do what I *suggested* to the guys in chapter seven. That was my soft sell. As we conclude our time together, I want to give you my hard sell.

Beginning today, take a year off all romantic and sexual pursuits.

As I said, I've been issuing this challenge for years. To my knowledge, no one has died or been seriously injured because of it. No one has reported that this sexual sabbatical was the worst year of his or her life. I've heard just the opposite. A twenty-two-year-old college student told me his year off probably saved his life. Every week—literally, every week—I get an email, letter, direct message, or mention from someone somewhere in the world telling me he just completed the one-year challenge. I've lost count of the people who've walked up and thanked me and then gone on to tell me about or introduce me to their husbands, wives, or fiancés, who, according to them, they would have never met had it not been for their year off. To be clear, I'm asking you to press pause on all things romantic or sexual for one year. No dates, no hooking up, no overnights, no nothing. Why *one* year? Because I don't think I can convince you to take two.

Clarity

The questions most frequently asked in relation to this year of unromantic living are:

What's to be gained?

What's the payoff?

What could be worth a year without sex?

The answer is *clarity*. Ladies, remember when you were

a bit younger and you went through your boy-crazy stage? Remember your momma warning you about certain kinds of boys and perhaps a few specific boys? Remember how you rolled your eyes and ignored her? Remember when it dawned on you that she was right? Your mother had two things you lacked as an adolescent: objectivity and experience. She had clarity. She was not stirred emotionally by the boys who kept skateboarding in front of your house. She'd lived long enough to know what they were up to.

Ever watched a friend make a relationship decision that was so obviously wrong you couldn't understand why he couldn't see it? You had something he didn't. Clarity. Clarity that stemmed from the fact you weren't emotionally or romantically involved with what's-her-name.

Three things contribute to moral clarity: objectivity, experience, and purity. Regarding sexual purity, let's be honest. Once a relationship gets physical, you lose objectivity. The more physical it gets, the less objective you become. If you've been in a series of relationships that went physical fast, you need a break. You need the clarity that a season of moral purity brings. This is true even if you have no intention of giving up sex until you're married. But I should warn you. Dozens of men and women have confided in me that they started their "romance fast" with serious doubts about their ability to make it through an entire year. But at the end of the year, they concluded that the relational objectivity and clarity they gained caused them to rethink their views on sex outside of marriage.

Filling the Time

If you are wondering what you're going to do with all that free time (and extra money), no worries. The one-year challenge actually has more to do with what you *do* during the year than it does with what you stop doing. Remember, the premise of this book is that it's more important to become someone than to find someone. The year off is an opportunity for you to focus your attention on *becoming the person the person you're looking for is looking for.* You think you can do both; you can date and change at the same time. But you can't. You've already tried. I bet you've promised yourself that you won't, you'll always, you'll never, you'll stop, and then you broke all your promises. Right? That's why you need a break. A twelve-month break.

To get the most out of your evenings at home and your weekends alone, there are five things I recommend you work on the entire year — three obvious ones based on the message of this book and two others I'll throw in for free. Here's the list, and then I'll elaborate on each:

- Address your past.
- Break some habits.
- Set some standards.
- Get out of debt.
- Go (back) to church.

Surprised?

Address the Past

For most people, moving forward requires a long, painful look back. If your family of origin was dysfunctional, and most are, this is the year to find someone to help you understand how your past intersects your future. The problem with unresolved relational issues is that they don't stay contained within the relationship of origin. They rear their ugly heads in future relationships. Bet you knew that. Bet you've seen that. So now is the time to develop the tools you need to ensure the past stays in the past. This is the year to acknowledge the pain you've been avoiding. This is the time to turn around and face down your history so it doesn't continue to reach out and sully your future.

If you aren't proactive, your past will smuggle itself into your future. Specifically, into future relationships. If there's someone you need to forgive, this is the year to do that. If there's someone waiting to hear you ask for forgiveness, now is the time. Use these twelve months to get healthy.

Break Some Habits

Odds are you've seen how a bad habit can negatively impact a romantic interest. Perhaps you had a ringside seat to the chaos that an unbridled appetite created in your parents' marriage. If you have a potential relationship-wrecking habit, now is the time to break it. Falling in love will not break you of bad habits. If you drink too much now, you'll drink too much then. If you've got a prescription drug addiction now, you'll have one then. If you hope to give yourself fully to someone in the future, now is the time to end your relationship with the substances and activities that own a piece of you. Whether alcohol, tobacco, drugs, gambling, porn, overspending, or overeating, ultimately it will undermine the trust and respect of the person you care about most. Most people don't address these types of things apart from the pressure of a relationship. Don't wait. Address them now. After all, isn't that what you hope the person you're hoping to meet 365 days from today is doing?

Guys, now is the time to break the habit of commoditizing women. This is the year to edit your playlist, reevaluate your watch list, and perhaps filter your Internet. Ladies, this is the year to stop allowing yourselves to be treated like commodities. Develop a high intolerance for anything but respect. You're going to hate me for saying this, but this is the year to stop dressing like a commodity. Do you know what determines a fisherman's choice of bait? The kind of fish he wants to catch. Ladies, if you fish with your bodies, you're going to catch body snatchers every single time. All men are not the same. If you think they are, it's because the men you've dated are all the same. But the common denominator in your last three relationships was ... you. While the man of your dreams is busy cleaning out his playlist, you may need to clean out your closet. Just sayin'. If you have to use your body to get him, you'll have to use your body to keep him. And as cute as you are today ...

Set Some Standards

During your year off, give serious thought to what you want your future relationships to look like regarding sexual involvement. To use an old youth-group adage, decide *how far is too far.* I know, as an adult it seems strange to think in those terms. But you know from experience that if you don't decide ahead of time, somebody will decide for you. Besides, why should someone else's lack of standards determine yours? So decide ahead of time. Pre-decide. A lack of self-control before marriage is often a foreshadowing of what happens after the dress is all boxed up. People who are sexually active before marriage are far more likely to be sexually unfaithful during marriage. Far more. Exercising self-control while dating is an investment in your own future. You're not giving up anything. You're investing in your most cherished relationship. Every time you say no, you're saying yes. Yes to intimacy. Yes to trust. Yes to a preferred future. Yes to a story you will be proud to tell. Yes to yourself.

So, how far is too far?

Here are three questions to help you decide:

- If your future love is out there somewhere wrestling with this same question, how would you want him or her to answer it?
- What level of physical involvement would lead you to lie about your past?
- What story do you want to tell?

Pre-decide. Be specific. Write it down. When your dating diet comes to an end, when you're ready to put yourself back on the market, share your new standards with a trusted friend. If that feels a bit too transparent, consider this. Everyone you dated in the past knows how far you were willing to go sexually. Your previous standards are not a secret. Now that you're moving forward, why not share your new standards with someone who can hold you accountable?

Get Out of Debt

People are always shocked that I include this on the list. But they shouldn't be. The number one source of conflict among couples is money. Financial pressure can suck the romance right out of a relationship. The primary source of financial pressure is debt. Dumb debt. Credit card debt. Car leases. Use this year to get out of debt. You may find it hard to believe, but you can get out of debt a lot quicker as a single than you can if you are in a relationship. Since you won't be going out for a year, you'll have extra cash to start paying off that credit card debt you accumulated in your attempt to impress all those folks who aren't even around anymore.

If you have debt, chances are you have other bad financial habits. Go ahead and add them to the bad-habit list you started a couple paragraphs ago. Debt is a pathway. It leads somewhere. This is the year to exit that path. You'll discover that lowering your standard of living will increase your quality of life. That's a lesson that will serve you well the rest of your life.

If you're thinking, *Andy, the person I'm looking for is a person who has the capacity to bail me out financially*, make sure to tell 'em up-front. First date. Say, "Look, I've got about nine grand in credit card debt. I'm looking for someone who's willing to pay that off for me. I don't plan to change my spending habits; I'm looking for someone to support my bad spending habits."

Far-fetched?

Let me ask you this. If it's okay for you to sneak your bad financial habits into a relationship, are you okay with him or her sneaking bad habits in as well? Or would you prefer to know up-front what you're dealing with? If you want to marry rich, knock yourself out. But in the meantime, get out of debt.

Go (Back) to Church

I told you earlier that when Sandra left home for college her mom told her, "If you go to the right places, you'll meet the right people." There's a lot of truth to that. Sandra and I met at a Bible study on the Georgia Tech campus. Neither of us was looking for a relationship. She had just ended one and I was happily single. We were both committed to whatever and whomever God had for us. We were raised to think that way. So we were at the right place and met the right person. I did anyway.

One of the right places where you may meet some right people is a good local church. Even if you don't consider yourself a church person, just try it. Find a church you enjoy.

It may take awhile. But keep looking. Start with the largest church in your community. There's a reason big churches are big. Generally they're good reasons. Don't be put off by the size; just get up and go. Sit close to the front. Bring a friend or two. If you enjoy the Sunday morning experience, look for an opportunity to get involved. Volunteer.

Remember, this is a year to become the person the person you're looking for is looking for. This is a year for renewing your mind and gaining moral clarity. This is the year to forgive and to ask for forgiveness. A good local church will support you in all those pursuits. So find a church you enjoy and get involved.

On the flip side, during your romance hiatus you may need to take a year off from some other locations. Which ones? The ones that immediately came to mind two sentences ago. The places that are likely to undermine your resolve. About three months in, you'll convince yourself you can handle it. But you can't. So just don't go. Pre-decide not to go.

So there's your to-do list:

- Address your past.
- Break some habits.
- Set some standards.
- Get out of debt.
- Go (back) to church.

Focus on those five things and these next twelve months will fly by. Well, they will go by. Actually, time may stand still. Either way, you may look back on this next year and consider it the most transformative year of your life. If so, you won't be the first. However ...

It Happens All the Time

One word of caution. Actually, it's more of a heads-up. A week or two after you make this commitment, you'll most likely meet the person you've been looking for. You'll be tempted to do with this commitment what you've done with previous commitments. Break it. But don't. You're not ready. You're not the person the person you're looking for is looking for. You need time. Remember what Denise's mother told her? "Sweetheart, the problem is, a guy like that is not looking for a girl like you." As painful as it is to read and consider, the same may be true for you. It's too early.

So break the wrist and walk away.

Several years after I first taught this content to our churches, I received the following email. It's a story of redemption. My prayer is that Stacy's story will be a catalyst for you to do what you know in your heart you need to do with what you've just read:

Hey Andy,

I assume you get a lot of these emails. So here's one more. I grew up in a broken home, and at the age of five, my mother and I moved five hundred miles away from my hometown. When I was twelve years old, I got "the talk," and while I do remember being encourgaed to wait until I found someone I loved, there was no encouragement to save sex until marriage. All I knew about sex was what my friends were doing, and this knowledge took me into my high school years with a constant state of numbness, giving myself away to every boyfriend I had.

During my first year of college, I began surrounding myself with different people. My new friends and I started attending Buckhead Church, and it became a routine for me to listen to your messages online. One night I found myself sitting in my dorm room listening to the first message in your series entitled, *Twisting the Truth*. I wasn't remotely prepared for what I was about to hear. I can remember everything about that night. It was a moment of truth in my life and my largest milestone to this day.

I was in tears, writing notes like a madman. I was slapped in the face with the truth about sex, and the shallowness of my relationship with God was revealed. I finally realized the connection between my experience with sex and my life of numbness. My intimacy factor was gone. Everything became real when you gave **the one-year challenge**. I had no idea how I was going to do that. But I printed out my notes, grabbed a pen, and wrote November 6, 2007. No dating for one year. No more sex until marriage. And then I signed it.

The very next day I wrote in my journal, *I made it one day, God*. It was the most challenging thing I had ever faced. There were so many guys floating around in my life. I had to cancel my text messaging. And slowly I began to feel sensitivity to my sin. Just one month after stepping up to the plate with God, I already began to feel him work in my heart. A few months later, an old high school acquaintance contacted me through Facebook. He noticed through my online bio that I had changed. He asked to hear my story, and I told him about my November 6 commitment.

When November 6, 2008 rolled around, he asked me out. I went, but after our date, I told him I just wanted to be friends. Four months passed, as well as a few dates with other people, and we ran into each other again. I was excited to see him. I had thought a lot about the lack of substance in the previous dates I had been on. We continued to talk and I slowly saw it all come together. I saw the beauty of what God wanted to do through our lives.

He was a virgin and had made the commitment when he was young to stay pure until marriage. I felt unworthy of that. He had a lifestyle that I desired but didn't feel deserving of. Our love story continued for a little over a year, and in July 2010, he asked me to marry him.

Our relationship is founded on friendship and faith. We set our marriage date exactly three years after God changed my life — Saturday, November 6, 2010. We just celebrated six months of marriage, and I'm in tears thinking of what we have been through. If it wasn't for the year thing and all God changed in my heart, not only would I be incapable of loving him the way he deserves to be loved, I probably wouldn't have him at all. We are so thankful to God for calling us into bigger stories than the ones we would have written for ourselves.

Thanks for listening,
Stacy

CONCLUSION

Recently I gathered with about 250 singles at one of our local churches to answer questions on the topic of love, sex, and dating. Attendees were asked to write their questions on cards and turn them in to the moderator ahead of time. The most pointed question of the night came from a middle-aged gentleman. His card read, "I'm divorced. Why save sex for marriage?" Good question. His direct question deserved a direct answer. I said, "If all there is to life is this life, if you are merely a predator and women are prey, if sex is just physical and disconnected from the concept of permanency, exclusivity, and relationship, then I can't think of a reason not to have sex with as many women as you can convince to hop into bed with you."

Not exactly the answer they were expecting from their pastor. My answer was particularly disturbing to women in the audience. Heck, it was particularly disturbing to me.

I let it sit for a moment and continued. "But if there's more to this life than what meets the eye ... if there is a God in whose image you've been made and in whose image every woman you've met has been made ... if sex was created with a purpose and if part of that purpose is to enhance the expression of intimacy between two people ... and if that fragile, wonderful, delicate experience we term *intimacy* can be damaged or broken through abuse, then your sexual conduct matters a great deal." Now women were crying and men were squirming. I continued. "So you have to decide what you believe. Not just about sex. About everything. Once you decide, the answer to your important question will be clear. Perhaps uncomfortably clear."

As you process the issues and questions surrounding your sexuality and expressions of your sexuality, don't forget the broader context. Sex isn't just physical. It's one component of a multifaceted biological, physiological, and psychological miracle that is *you*. So cherish it. Protect it. Preserve it. Reserve it. I've never met anyone who exercised self-control in the area of sexuality who regretted it later. We both know people who didn't, and do.

One question that wasn't asked during that particular Q&A session is a question that's almost always asked when people can ask anonymously: *Is it ever too late?* Is there a point of no return? A point at which too much damage is done and it's futile to try to correct it?

Again, the answer to that question hinges on your worldview, what you believe. As a follower of Jesus, I'm convinced restoration, renewal, and redemption are available to all of us regardless of what we have done or what was done to us. The question behind the question is, *Is there hope?* Yes. There's hope. There's a way back. The way back begins with your decision to become someone rather than merely meet someone. The way back begins with your decision to write a better story, a story you would be proud to tell your children or grandchildren. Those are decisions you can make today. Right now. Those decisions ensure the next chapter will be better than the previous one.

I hope you fall in love and stay there. I hope you get the opportunity to commit yourself to someone *prepared* to commit to you in return. You have no control over when or if you'll meet your right person. What you *can* control is what you do in the meantime. So, *become the person the person you're looking for is looking for.* Prepare to commit. Who knows, there may be someone out there preparing for you as well.

NOTES

1. About 50 percent of first marriages, 67 percent of second marriages, and 73 percent of third marriages end in divorce ("The Intelligent Divorce," *Psychology Today*, February 6, 2012).

2. Krystle Russin, "Saving Marriage: Having a Baby Isn't Going to Help Your Relationship, Experts Say" (www.divorce360.com).

3. Sarah Harris, "The Argument for Marriage: Unwed Parents Are Six Times More Likely to Split Up By the Time Their Child Is Five: (*Daily Mail Online*, June 17, 2011).

4. *ABC News*, January 28, 2014.

5. *The Washington Times*, April 23, 2011.

6. For a full explanation of the de-elevated status of women in ancient Roman and Jewish culture, see chapter four of *How Christianity Changed the World*, by Alvin J. Schmidt (Zondervan, 2004).

7. For a detailed account of the influence and elevated status of women in the early church, see chapter five of *The Rise of Christianity*, by Rodney Stark (HarperOne, 1997).

8. While there is disagreement among interpreters of Matthew 19:5 – 6 as to whether "be united" or "one flesh" refers to sexual union, it is safe to assume Jesus assumed sexual intercourse between husbands and wives based on his teaching in the same passage that a woman who remarries commits adultery. Adultery would assume sexual intercourse with her new husband.

9. *Pro Caelio*, a speech from Marcus Tullius Cicero in defense of Marcus Caelius Rufus, one of Cicero's former students and political rivals (Section 48).

SMALL GROUP VIDEO DISCUSSION GUIDE

This discussion guide was developed for use with *The New Rules for Love, Sex, and Dating* four-session video, which complements and expands the material in this book. Ideally, those leading a group discussion on *The New Rules for Love, Sex, and Dating* should preview each video session and read through the accompanying portion of the discussion guide before the group meets. While the material in the discussion guide is intended for use with the video, some of the discussion questions will also reflect content used in the book.

The four video sessions cover the overarching themes of the book and are:

1. The Right Person Myth
2. Gentleman's Club
3. Designer Sex
4. If I Were You

FORMAT OF THE DISCUSSION GUIDE

- **Introduction and Opening Question**—Each session features a short introduction to establish the theme. If your group wants to open with a question that serves as a discussion starter or icebreaker, please make use of this question.

- **Video Viewing**—The video clip for each session is approximately 15–20 minutes.

- **Video Discussion**—These questions are designed to follow Andy's video teaching and engage the group in discussion around the content they just watched. Some of the questions focus on specific Bible passages used in the video and tie in with the theme of the session.

- **Moving Forward**—This challenge helps group members consider how they might put what they learned into action.

- **Between Sessions**—Each session concludes with a key Bible passage to memorize as well as recommended reading from the book to prepare for the next meeting.

SESSION 1: **The Right Person Myth**

INTRODUCTION

The Right Person Myth says, *If I marry the right person, every-thing will be all right.*

That's what many married people told themselves when they were single. Then they set off looking for the right person. They met someone they were physically attracted to, added sex to the relationship right away, and fell into a kind of neuro-chemical bliss that made them believe that not only had they never loved like this, *no one in human history* had.

But once they got married, they had a problem: all their marriage had going for it was chemistry. Neither the husband nor the wife knew anything about relationships. Soon enough, their relationship problems began causing chemistry problems. The sexual part of the marriage died, leaving both of them frustrated and confused. So one or both of them decided that maybe he didn't marry "the right person" after all. Separation and divorce followed.

The good news is that marriage doesn't have to be like that. There's a different way—a better way. Our culture doesn't celebrate this different way because it's boring. No one wants to watch a movie about a happily married couple. There isn't enough drama. Fairy tales end with "and they lived happily ever after" because actually watching two people live happily ever after would be like watching paint dry. But there's noth-ing boring about actually living happily ever after—and you can, provided you come to understand that "happily ever after" requires preparation and changing your mind-set.

Think about some popular movies, TV shows, and songs about romance. What do they indicate about our culture's current rules regarding love, sex, and dating? Which of the rules do you agree with? Which ones do you disagree with?

VIDEO VIEWING AND NOTES

Watch the session 1 video, "The Right Person Myth," as a group and note anything that impacts you.

VIDEO DISCUSSION

1. Do you agree that the "right person myth" is indeed a myth? How have you seen this way of thinking affect your relationships or those of your friends?

2. Read 1 Corinthians 13:4–5. Which of the qualities mentioned is most difficult for you to exhibit? Which quality do you value most in the people you date? Why?

3. Briefly list the qualities of the person you're currently dating (or a person you'd like to date). Then briefly list the qualities of the person you'd like to marry. Are the qualities in the two lists the same? If not, why not?

4. Consider the "person you'd like to marry" list you just made. What kind of guy or girl do you think *that* person is looking for?

5. Are you spending more time looking for the right person or becoming the right person? Explain.

MOVING FORWARD

If you date with the idea that you're on a quest for the right person, you're setting yourself up for failure. Healthy relationships don't result from pursuing desirable qualities on a checklist. You'll never mysteriously, providentially run into the right person. You don't need to *find* the right person. You need to *become* the right person.

What's one step you can take this week to start becoming the person the person you're looking for is looking for?

BETWEEN SESSIONS

1. Memorize these key verses during the coming week:

   Love is patient, love is kind. It does not envy, it does not boast, it is not proud. It does not dishonor others, it is not self-seeking, it is not easily angered, it keeps no record of wrongs.

   (1 CORINTHIANS 13:4–5)

2. Read the introduction and chapters 1–5 of this book.

SESSION 2: **Gentleman's Club**

INTRODUCTION

"Sex sells." That's what we're told, right? It's possible to sell just about anything if you associate it with images of scantily clad women. Some companies even use sex to sell website hosting, maybe one of the least inherently sexy products imaginable.

But why does sex sell? Like it or not, men continue to set the pace for culture and relationships. Consequently, they're responsible for the way women are depicted in movies, television, and advertisements. Sadly, in our culture women are viewed, presented, talked about, and sung about as commodities —objects to be used without forming attachments. "Take me, use me, do whatever you want with me, and then trade me in," airbrushed and photo-shopped models seem to say from ad pages and TV commercials.

Last session, we exploded the right person myth and talked about the importance of becoming who the person the person you're looking for is looking for. One of the Bible verses we looked at was 1 Corinthians 13:11: "When I was a child, I talked like a child, I thought like a child, I reasoned like a child. When I became a man, I put the ways of childhood behind me." Our culture's dehumanizing view of women has left many men thinking like little boys. If you're a single guy, this session's content has the potential to change your way thinking and set you up for relational success.

If you're a woman (or a group of women), it's important to understand that even though much of what we'll discuss this session is aimed more at men, you need to change the way you think too. It's inevitable that the way men think about women has influenced to one degree or another the way you think about yourself.

Who is a woman you'd be honored to meet? Why would you want to meet her?

VIDEO VIEWING AND NOTES

Watch the session 2 video, "Gentleman's Club," as a group and note anything that impacts you.

VIDEO DISCUSSION

1. Do you agree with Andy's observation that women are viewed as commodities in our culture? If so, what evidence do you see? How has that cultural belief crept into your own mind-set?

2. **Men:** How does what men learn from the "school of porn" contrast with how Jesus, Paul, and Peter told men to treat women? Do you think pornography could have lasting negative effects on your relationships with women? Why or why not?

Women: What lessons do women learn from the "school of porn"? How does the prevalence of erotic imagery in our society affect women's self-images and sense of self-worth?

3. **Men:** Think back to the woman you said you'd be honored to meet. How would you act in her presence? What would it look like if you treated all women with that kind of respect?

Women: Think back to a time when you felt honored by a man. How did he treat you differently from most men in your life?

4. **Men:** How does the way men treat women affect how women view themselves? What burden of responsibility does that place on men?

Women: Do you think the way women treat men affects how men view themselves? How so?

5. What are some qualities you need to develop to become the person the person you're looking for is looking for?

MOVING FORWARD

For Men: The words of Jesus, Paul, and Peter are your targets. You need to embrace these fundamental truths and treat women accordingly. Honor them. This applies to the women you're attracted to, the women you're not attracted to, and the women you date and dump.

For Women: The creator of the universe is your heavenly Father. You are his daughter. If you're not being treated as such, it's not a reflection of the value God places on you, and it's not acceptable.

To change the way you view yourself, you need to *renew your mind* (Romans 12:2). This means bringing your thoughts and behaviors in line with God's values, not culture's.

What is one thing you can do this week to begin to renew your mind?

BETWEEN SESSIONS

1. Memorize these key verses during the coming week:

   "A new command I give you: Love one another. As I have loved you, so you must love one another. By this everyone will know that you are my disciples, if you love one another."

   (JOHN 13:34–35)

2. Read chapters 6–7 of this book.

SESSION 3: **Designer Sex**

INTRODUCTION

In session 1, we talked about the right person myth. This session we're discuss another of our cultural myths: *sex—it's only physical*. We all know intuitively that this isn't true, but our culture usually ignores evidence to the contrary.

If sex is only physical, why do children who are sexually abused find it so difficult to shake off the abuse, even as adults? Why does it follow them throughout their lives? If sex is only physical, why is rape so much more devastating to women than being beaten up? If sex is only physical, why do men with the deepest sexual issues usually have uninvolved or disconnected fathers? If sex is only physical, why are most people's greatest regrets sexual?

If you live as though sex is only physical, it will come back to haunt you. You'll hurt yourself emotionally and spiritually. If you get married, you'll hurt your spouse. You'll have to live with the consequences of your poor sexual decisions.

If someone younger than you asked for just one piece of advice about sex, what would you tell him or her? And how would you define the purpose of sex?

VIDEO VIEWING AND NOTES

Watch the session 3 video, "Designer Sex," as a group and note anything that impacts you.

VIDEO DISCUSSION

1. Do you agree with the idea that sex isn't just physical? Why or why not?

2. Paul defined sexual immorality as sex outside of marriage. Do you agree? In what ways is this standard trivialized in today's culture?

3. Read 1 Corinthians 6:18. What does it look like in our culture to "flee" sexual immorality?

4. Read 1 Corinthians 6:19–20. How does this view of our bodies affect what we should believe and practice when it comes to sex?

5. What's okay for you to do sexually? What's not? What's okay for your future spouse to do sexually?

MOVING FORWARD

Sex is a source of great pleasure, but it can also be a source of great pain. You have an opportunity to get things right by laying a solid foundation for marriage. It requires a commitment to trust God and delay gratification for something much better in the future.

To become the person the person you're looking for is looking for, you need to commit to live the kind of story *now* that person will want to hear *later*—the kind of story that shows you chose to honor him or her before you'd even met.

What story do you want to tell your spouse one day?

BETWEEN SESSIONS

1. Memorize this key verse during the coming week:

    Flee from sexual immorality. All other sins a person commits are outside the body, but whoever sins sexually, sins against their own body.

    (1 CORINTHIANS 6:18)

2. Read chapters 8–9 of this book.

SESSION 4: **If I Were You**

Marriage is a goal that many of us hope for in our lives. But before marriage comes dating. Dating is a time when you can get to know a person better. And the choices you make during this time can often make or break the relationship. So, what kind of choices does it take now to say "I do" and mean it later?

For starters, we have to realize that the past is a better indicator than a promise. How you live your life really matters. The choices you make throughout your life reveal the kind of person you are becoming. Did you know that the paths you choose trump the commitments you make? If you are going to commit to becoming someone who can keep commitments later, then the choices you have made and the choices you make now need to be seriously considered.

So, here is a challenge: consider taking a year off all romantic and sexual pursuits. During this "one year challenge," think about some of the following things:

- *Address your past.* If you get married without seriously dealing with your childhood issues, they will show up over and over and over. This will not only put a strain on your future marriage but could derail it.

- *Break some habits.* Don't dress like a commodity or put up with being treated like one. You are more than a body— you have a brain, goals, passions. Make sure that in any relationship you are valued as a whole person and that you are deeply respected. Be careful of dressing in a way that attracts longing looks, but rather present yourself in a way that gives you dignity and worth.

- *Get out of debt.* No one wants to enter a marriage with financial indebtedness. The fewer loans and bills that you take into a marriage, the more financial stability you can begin your relationship with. Attempt to pay off everything you owe before you decide to get married.

What are choices you can make that will prepare you to say "I do" and really mean it?

VIDEO VIEWING AND NOTES

Watch the session 4 video, "If I Were You," as a group and note anything that impacts you.

VIDEO DISCUSSION

1. Do you agree that "the past is a better indicator than a promise"? If so, how will that factor into your dating decisions moving forward?

2. Did you read or hear anything during this session that resonates with you? Explain.

3. Read Proverbs 14:15. What warning signs might an in-love couple ignore because love makes us prone to believe anything? What can you do in your own relationships to pay attention to these warning signs?

4. What are some of the potential consequences of bringing your unresolved past into marriage? What childhood issues do you need to resolve in order to spare your future spouse from having to deal with them later?

5. Do you think there are specific ways a woman should present herself to attract a prudent man? In what ways are men responsible for how they respond to how a woman dresses?

MOVING FORWARD

God didn't design marriage to fix people's flaws. In fact, our flaws are often magnified in marriage. So why not start now becoming the person your future spouse wants and needs? Your preparation now is worth much more than your commitment later.

Consider taking the year-off challenge. During this time, pick an area of your life — debt, unresolved past issues, bad habits, dress, boundaries—and set a goal. Then list the steps that will put you on a path toward achieving that goal and becoming the person the person you're looking for is looking for.

Thinking back over the four sessions of this study, what's your number-one takeaway—the one thing you learned that you're most eager to apply? Why?

IN THE COMING DAYS

1. Memorize this key verse during the coming week:

   The simple believe anything, but the prudent give thought to their steps.

   (PROVERBS 14:8)

2. Read chapter 10 and the conclusion of this book.